MW00910427

dBASE 5.0
for Windows

Timothy J. O'Leary
Linda I. O'Leary

3 4 5 6 7 8 9 0 BAN BAN 9 0 9 8 7 6

ISBN 0-07-049037-6

Library of Congress Catalog Card Number 94-78316

Information has been obtained by McGraw-Hill from sources believed to be reliable. However, because of the possibility of human or mechanical error by our sources, McGraw-Hill, or others, McGraw-Hill does not guarantee the accuracy, adequacy, or completeness of any information and is not responsible for any errors or omissions or the results obtained from use of such information.

CONTENTS

Overview Database DB3
Definition of a Database   DB3
Advantages of Using a Database   DB4
Database Terminology   DB4
Case Study for Labs 1–4   DB5
Before You Begin   DB5
Instructional Conventions   DB6

Lab 1 Creating a Database Using dBASE 5.0 for Windows DB7
Loading dBASE 5.0 for Windows   DB7
Exploring the dBASE Application
    Window   DB8
Creating a Database   DB9
Planning a Database   DB10
Creating a New Table   DB11
Using Help   DB13
Defining the Table Structure   DB15
Saving the Table Structure   DB21
Entering Data   DB22
Viewing Records   DB30
Printing a Table   DB34
Exiting dBASE   DB35
Key Terms   DB35
Command Summary   DB36
Lab Review   DB36
Matching   DB36
Fill-In Questions   DB37
Practice Exercises   DB38

Lab 2 Working with Tables and Designing a Custom Form DB43
Using the Navigator   DB43
Editing Data   DB47
Replacing Record Values   DB49
Deleting Records   DB52
Locating Information in a Table   DB54
Restructuring a Table   DB57
Freezing a Field   DB59
Sorting Records   DB61
Indexing a Table   DB65
Updating Indexed Tables   DB69
Creating a Customized Form   DB70

Selecting and Moving Objects   DB73
Enhancing the Form   DB77
Adding Objects to a Form   DB79
Entering Data in the Custom
    Form   DB81
Key Terms   DB83
Command Summary   DB83
Lab Review   DB84
Matching   DB84
Practice Exercises   DB84

Lab 3 Querying Database Tables DB89
Querying a Table   DB89
Moving Columns   DB93
Querying with Wildcards   DB94
Querying Using Comparison
    Operators   DB97
Using Logical ANDs and ORs   DB98
Querying Two Tables   DB100
Querying for an Exact Match   DB106
Querying Three Tables   DB107
Creating a Calculated Field   DB109
Creating a Multitable Form   DB113
Key Terms   DB119
Command Summary   119
Lab Review   DB120
Matching   DB120
Practice Exercises   DB120

Lab 4 Reporting Data Using Crystal Reports DB123
Designing a Report   DB123
Previewing the Report   DB129
Editing Text Fields   DB131
Adding Text Fields   DB134
Aligning Objects   DB136
Sorting the Report   DB137
Creating a Multitable Report   DB138
Grouping the Report   DB140
Enhancing the Report   DB145
Creating a Report with a Calculated
    Field   DB148
Creating Totals   DB149

Changing Margins   DB153
Creating a Catalog   DB154
Key Terms   DB156
Command Summary   DB156
Lab Review   DB157
Matching   DB157
Practice Exercises   DB157

Case Project DB159
Final Project   DB159
Part I   DB159
Part II   DB160
Part III   DB160

Summary dBASE 5.0 for Windows DB161
Glossary of Key Terms   DB161
Summary of Selected dBASE 5.0 for
    Windows Commands   DB164

Index DB167

Database

A word processor helps you enter and manipulate text. An electronic spreadsheet helps you enter and analyze numerical data. A computerized database helps you enter and manage information or data in record format.

Databases have been in existence for many years. Paper records organized in a filing cabinet by name or department are a database. The information in a telephone book, organized alphabetically, is a database. A school's records of teachers, classes, and students are collectively a database.

Before computers, most database records were kept on paper. With computers, the same data is entered and stored on a disk. The big difference is that an electronic database can manipulate—sort, analyze, and display—the data quickly and efficiently. What took hours of time to pull from the paper files can be extracted in a matter of seconds using a computerized database.

Definition of a Database

A *database* is an organized collection of related data that is stored in a file. The data is entered as a record that consists of several fields of data. Each record contains the same fields. For example, a school has a database of student records. Each record may contain the following fields of data: name, address, Social Security number, phone number, classes, and grades. All the records for each student in the school are stored in a file.

Some database programs only access and manipulate the data in a single file. Others allow the user to access and relate several files at one time. For example, the school may have a second database file containing data for each student's current class schedule. At the end of the semester the grades are posted in this file for each student. The data in one file can then be linked to the data in another file by using a common field, such as the student's name. The ability to link database files creates a relational database. Relational databases allow you to create smaller and more manageable database files, since you can combine and extract data between files.

The database program contains commands that allow the user to design the structure of the database records and enter the data for each record into the file. This is the physical storage of the data. How this data is retrieved, organized, and manipulated is the conceptual use of the data.

DATABASE

Advantages of Using a Database

A computerized database system does not save time by making the data quicker to enter. This, as in most programs, is a function of the typing speed of the user and his or her knowledge of the program.

One of the main advantages to using a computerized database system is the ability to quickly locate specific records. Once data is entered into the database file, you can quickly search the database to locate a specific record based on the data in a field. In a manual system, a record can usually be located by knowing one key piece of information. For example, if the records are stored in a file cabinet alphabetically by last name, to quickly find a record you must know the last name. In a computerized database, even if the records are sorted or organized by last name, you can still quickly locate a record using information in another field.

A computerized database also makes it easy to add and delete records from the file. Once a record is located, you can edit the contents of the fields to update the record or delete the record entirely from the file. You can also add new records to a file. When the record is entered, it is automatically placed in the correct organizational location within the file.

Another advantage of using a computerized database system is its ability to arrange the records in the file according to different fields of data. The records can be organized by name, department, pay, class, or whatever else is needed at a particular time. This ability to produce multiple file arrangements helps provide more meaningful information. The same records can provide information to different departments for different purposes.

A fourth advantage is the ability to perform calculations on different fields of data. Instead of pulling each record from a filing cabinet, recording the piece of data you want to use, and then calculating a record for the total field, you can simply have the database program sum all the values in the specified field. Additionally, you can instruct the program to select only certain records that meet specific conditions to be used in the calculations. Information that was once costly and time-consuming to get is now quickly and readily available.

Another advantage of database programs is the ability to quickly produce reports ranging from simple listings to complex, professional-looking reports. A simple report can be created by asking for a listing of specified fields of data and restricting the listing to records meeting specified conditions. A more complex, professional report can be created using the same restrictions or conditions as the simple report, but the data can be displayed in different layout styles, and can display titles, headings, subtotals, and totals.

In manual systems, there are often several files containing some of the same data. A computerized database system can allow access by more than one department to the same data. Common updating of the data can be done by any department. The elimination of duplicate information saves both space and time.

Database Terminology

Database: An organized collection of related data.

Delete: To remove a record from the database file.

Edit: To change or update the data in a field.

Field: A collection of related characters, such as last name.

File: A database of records.

Record: A collection of related fields, such as class time, class name, or grade.

Relational database: Database files that have a common field and can be linked to extract and combine data from multiple files.

Report: A listing of specified fields of data for specified records in the file.

Search: To locate a specific record in a file.

Sort: To arrange the records in a file in a specified order.

Case Study for Labs 1–4

As a recent college graduate, you have accepted your first job with The Sports Company, a chain of sporting goods stores located throughout the United States. The company has recently purchased dBASE 5.0 for Windows and you have been assigned the job of updating their current record-keeping system for employee records.

Lab 1   In the first lab you will learn how to design and create the structure for a computerized database and how to enter and edit records in the database. You will also print a simple report of the records you enter in the database file.

Lab 2   You will continue to build, modify, and use the employee database of records. You will learn how to sort and index the records in a database file to make it easier to locate records. Additionally, you will create a customized data entry form to make it easier to enter and edit data in the database file.

Lab 3   In this lab you will learn how to query the database to locate specific information. Additionally, you will learn how to use and link multiple tables, create calculated fields, and create a multitable form.

Lab 4   In this lab you will learn how to use Crystal Reports to create weekly and monthly employee status reports. You will use multiple files to create several different reports. The reports will display selected fields of data for the records in the database. They will also include report titles, subgroupings of data, and descriptive text to clarify the meaning of the data in the reports.

Before You Begin

The following assumptions have been made:

- dBASE 5.0 for Windows has been properly installed on the hard disk of your computer system in the directory DBASEWIN and the default program settings are in effect.

- The data disk contains the data files needed to complete the series of labs and practice exercises. These files should be on the root directory of your disk and are supplied by your instructor.

- The drive you are using for your data disk is drive A.

- You have completed the DOS and Windows labs or you are already familiar with basic DOS and Windows terminology and procedures.

Instructional Conventions

The command sequences you are to issue will appear on a single line following the word "Choose." Each command selection will be separated by a >. If the menu command can be selected by typing a letter of the command, the letter will appear bold and underlined. Anything you are to type will also appear in bold text. You can use either the keyboard or mouse to enter the commands. If there is a keyboard shortcut for the command, it will appear below the command preceded by a ➢ symbol. If there is a mouse alternative to the command, it will appear following the word "Click."

1 Creating a Database Using dBASE 5.0 for Windows

CASE STUDY

As a recent college graduate, you have accepted your first job as a management trainee with The Sports Company. This company consists of a chain of sporting goods stores located in large metropolitan areas across the United States. The stores are warehouse oriented, discounting the retail price of most items 15 percent. They stock sporting goods products for all the major sports: basketball, football, tennis, aerobics, and so on.

Your training program emphasis is on computer applications related to retail management. You have been assigned to the Southwest regional office as an assistant to the Regional Manager. The company has recently purchased dBASE for Windows, a database applications program. Your primary responsibility is to use dBASE to update the current system of maintaining employee records.

In this lab you will learn how to design a database for the employee records and create the structure for the database table using dBASE 5.0 for Windows.

Competencies

After completing this lab, you will know how to:

1. Load dBASE 5.0 for Windows.
2. Plan and create a database.
3. Use Help.
4. Define a table structure.
5. Save a table structure.
6. Enter data.
7. View records.
8. Print a table.
9. Exit dBASE for Windows.

DATABASE

Loading dBASE 5.0 for Windows

You must start dBASE 5.0 for Windows from the Windows 3.1 (or later) environment.
Start Windows. If necessary refer to Lab 1 in your Windows tutorial for startup instructions or consult your instructor.

The Windows Program Manager should display the dBASE for Windows group icon ▦ .
dBASE 5.0

Note: If your system is set up differently, your instructor will provide alternative instructions.

Put your data disk in drive A (or the appropriate drive for your system). Open the dBASE for Windows group window. Choose the dBASE for Windows program-item icon 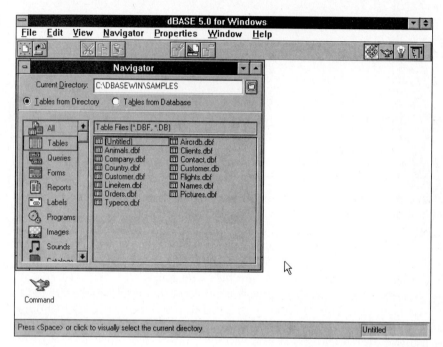.

Note: If a System error box appears indicating that the program cannot read from a drive, press [Esc] to choose Cancel, then press [←Enter] to choose OK.

A title screen is displayed while the computer loads the dBASE for Windows program into memory. After a few moments, the dBASE application window is displayed. If necessary, maximize the dBASE for Windows application window.
Your screen should be similar to Figure 1-1.

FIGURE 1-1

Exploring the dBASE Application Window

When you start dBASE, the application window is opened with the Navigator window open inside it. As you can see, there are many dBASE for Windows features that are common to the Windows environment. Among those features are a title bar, menu bar, control-menu boxes, minimize and maximize/restore buttons, icons, and mouse compatibility. You can move and size dBASE windows, select commands, use Help, and switch between files and programs just like in all other Windows applications. Your knowledge of how to use Windows makes learning about and using dBASE for Windows much easier.

The Navigator window may be in a different location and a different size than in Figure 1-1.

The **menu bar** displays the titles of the currently available menus. The menus contain commands you can choose to open windows, configure your screen, and work with your data. The menu bar contains only the menus you need at the moment. If a menu is not appropriate for a given task, it does not appear on the menu bar.

In addition, the window displays a **SpeedBar**. The SpeedBar contains buttons that represent shortcuts for common menu commands and faster methods for navigating through information in the database. The SpeedBar buttons can only be used if you have a mouse. You will learn about using these buttons shortly.

The last line in the application window is the **status bar**. It provides information about the task you are working on and the current state of operation or **mode** that dBASE is using. Like the menu bar and the SpeedBar, the appearance of the status bar changes as you work.

The large area between the SpeedBar and status bar is the **desktop**. This area displays different windows that are used to create and manipulate database files. The desktop currently displays the Navigator window and the Command window icon ❧. The **Navigator** window is used to access and organize your database files. You will learn how to use the Navigator throughout the labs. The **Command window** icon is displayed because this window is open, but minimized. The Command window displays the dBASE language commands that execute when you perform actions using the program.

All the features in dBASE that allow you to interact with the program are called the **user interface**. These features include menus, SpeedBar buttons, dialog boxes, and many other graphical elements you will be learning about throughout the labs.

If you have a mouse attached to your computer, the mouse pointer ⬉ is displayed on the screen. The mouse operates just as in Windows. You will learn about using the mouse specifically in dBASE for Windows throughout the labs.

Creating a Database

A **database** is an organized collection of information. For example, the information in your address book is a database. dBASE stores the information in tables. A **table** consists of vertical columns and horizontal rows of information. A row in a table contains data about an individual person, place, or thing. Each row is called a record. A **record** is a collection of related information, such as a person's name, address, and phone number.

Each piece of related information in a record is contained in a column, called a field. A **field** is a collection of related characters, such as persons' names.

dBASE is a **relational database** program. This means that you can define a **relation** between tables by having a common field in the tables. The common field lets you create a link between the tables so you can extract and combine data from multiple tables. You will learn more about relational databases in Lab 3.

A simple example of a database is shown below. This database consists of two tables of data, a Customer table and an Orders table. The Customer table contains information about the customers, such as their names and addresses. It also contains a field called Customer No., which contains a number that uniquely identifies each customer. The Orders table contains data about the orders placed by each customer, such as the date of order, order number, and customer number. The Customer Number field is the common field used to create a link between the two tables.

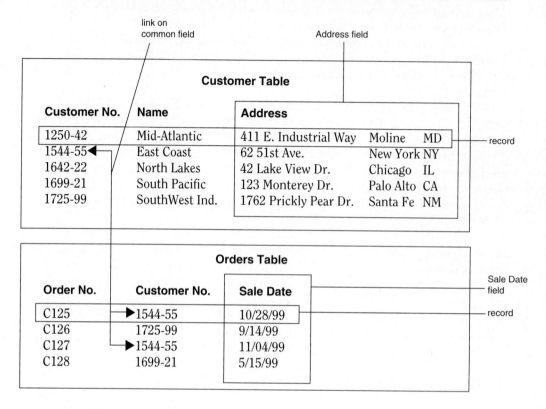

Planning a Database

The Sports Company plans to use dBASE to maintain several different types of databases. The database you will create will contain information about each Sports Company employee. Other plans for using dBASE include keeping track of preferred customers and inventory.

Your first step is to plan the design of your database. You need to decide what information each table in the employee database should contain and how it should be structured or laid out.

This information can be obtained by analyzing the current record-keeping procedures used throughout the company. It is important to understand the existing procedures so that your database tables reflect the information that is maintained by different departments. You should be aware of the forms that are the basis for the data entered into their records and of the information that is taken from their records to produce periodic reports. You also need to find out what information they would like to be able to obtain from the database that may be too difficult to generate using their current procedures.

After looking over the existing record-keeping procedures and the reports that are created from the information, you decide to create several tables of data that have the employee number as the common field to link the tables. Creating several smaller tables of related data rather than one large table makes it easier to use the tables and faster to process data. This is because you can link several tables together as needed.

Creating a New Table

The first database table you will create will include all the personal information on an employee, such as name, address, and date of birth. This data is currently maintained in the employee's personnel folder.

After carefully looking at the data in the personnel folders and the reports that are generated from this data, you need to decide how to break the information into fields. How you set up the database affects what you can do with the information in the database later on. For example, you could include the employees' first and last names in one field in the table. However, a table designed this way is hard to arrange and makes locating information difficult because too much information is included in one field. Alternatively, you could set up two fields for the same information, one for each part of the name. The advantage to creating separate and smaller fields of information is the flexibility it gives you later on to locate and arrange information.

You decide to include the fields shown below:

> Employee #
> Hire Date
> Last Name
> First Name
> Street
> City
> State
> Zip Code
> Birth Date

Now that you have decided upon the fields of data you want to include in the table, you are ready to create a new table by specifying the characteristics of the table.

To create a new table, the SpeedBar button or the New command on the File menu is used. Follow either the mouse or keyboard instructions below, as appropriate.

The SpeedBar buttons allow you to use the mouse to activate many dBASE commands without using the menu.

To find out what each button does, point to each button on the SpeedBar and read the short description in the status bar.

The first button on the left of the SpeedBar is the Create a New File button. To use the button to create a new table,

Click: New File

DATABASE

Choose: File>New

A menu of eight options is displayed. Each option lets you create a different type of dBASE file. To create a new database table file,

Choose: Table

Your screen should be similar to Figure 1-2.

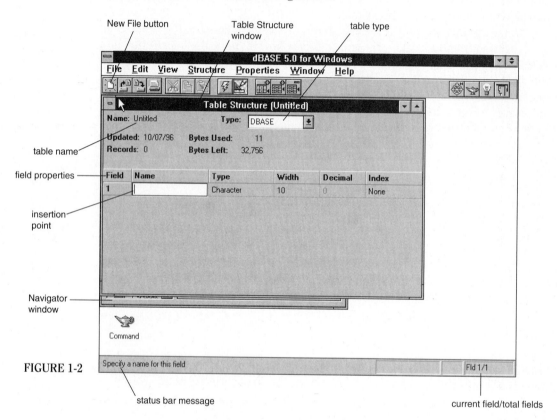

FIGURE 1-2

The Table Designer is open and displays the Table Structure window. The Table Designer is used to create new tables and to modify existing tables. The Table Structure window is displayed over the Navigator window. The default table name Untitled is displayed in the window title bar. This window is used to define the table **structure**, or the specifications and arrangement of fields in a table. The table structure consists of the name and type of table and the name and description of each field in the table.

The Table Structure window is made up of two main areas. The top area describes the following properties that apply to the entire table:

Name   The name of the table, or "Untitled" if the table has not yet been saved.

Type   The type of table, either dBASE (default) or Paradox. dBASE supports dBASE and Paradox file formats that allow you to create tables in formats that are accepted by other database programs.

Updated   The date the table was last updated and saved. The date on your computer system should be displayed here, since this is a new table.

Record   The number of records in the table.

Bytes Used   The total number of bytes used by the *fields* defined in the table.

Bytes Left   The maximum *record* size for the selected table type, minus the bytes used. dBASE records can be up to 32,767 bytes.

> The default is a setting that has been preselected by the program.

The lower portion of the Table Structure window is used to define the properties of the fields in the table. Because this is a new table, there are no fields defined. Each row in the table structure represents a field and each column shows the field's properties. The field properties include a field number, field name, field type, width, decimal, and an index. The field number displays 1, in anticipation that you will define the first field. The Name column of the first field is highlighted, indicating that it is selected. The insertion point (the blinking vertical bar) indicates that the Table Designer is ready to accept the field name for the first field.

The application window status bar displays a brief message on how to proceed. Since the Name column is selected, the description indicates that you need to specify a name for the field. The right end of the status bar displays "Fld 1/1." This shows that the highlight is positioned on the first field of a total of one field in the table.

Using Help

For more information about field names, you will use the dBASE Help system. As in Windows, the Help system is context-sensitive. This means dBASE will display Help information about the currently highlighted menu command or window. Since the Name column is selected, Help will provide information on this topic. Help can be accessed by pressing the Help key, F1 .

For Help on field names,

Press: F1 HELP

Your screen should be similar to Figure 1-3.

FIGURE 1-3

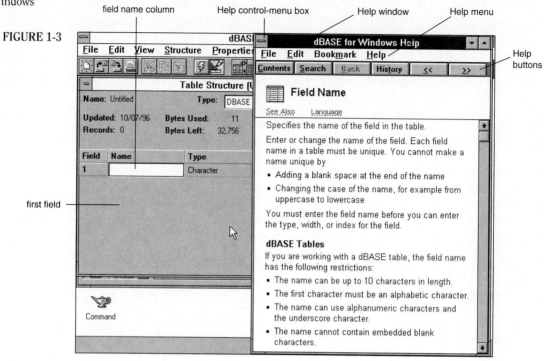

The Help window presents information about the rules governing dBASE field names. The Help system in dBASE for Windows is a separate application and works the same as Help in Windows. The Help menu contains commands that can be used in Help, and the Help buttons enable you to move around easily in Help.

Read the information about dBASE field names on this screen. Then,

Choose:	File>Exit
➤	Alt + F4
or	
Double-click:	Help control-menu box

You have exited the Help system and the window is closed.

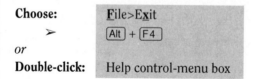

Use the scroll bar or ↓ to scroll the Help window to read the information that is not currently visible in the window.

Shortcut keys will appear below the command, preceded by a ➤ symbol.

Defining the Table Structure

As you learned from Help, a field name should be descriptive of the contents of the data to be entered in the field. It can be up to 10 characters long and can consist of letters, numbers, and underscores. The name must begin with an alphabetic character and cannot include any blank spaces. The name must be entered before you can specify the other field properties.

The first field of data you will enter in the table is the employee number. The employee number field will contain a four-digit number that is assigned to each employee when hired. Each new employee is given the next consecutive number, therefore no two employees can have the same four digits.

You have decided to name the first field "EMP_NUMBER." The name can be typed in either uppercase or lowercase letters. dBASE will display the characters of the field name in all uppercase letters. To enter the first field name,

Type: emp_number

As you type, the insertion point moves to show your location in the column.

Since the data you will enter in this field is a maximum of four characters, you decide to shorten the field name to EMP_NUM, so the field name is closer in size to the data that will be entered in the field. To correct the entry, you will delete the characters "BER." The (Backspace) key will delete characters to the left of the insertion point.

To correct the entry, use (Backspace) to erase the letters "BER."

Your screen should be similar to Figure 1-4.

> You can have up to 1024 fields in a table.

> dBASE will not accept an entry of illegal characters.

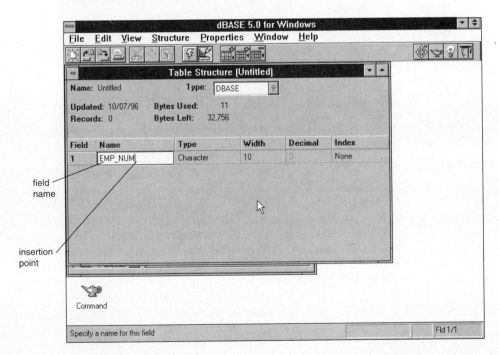

FIGURE 1-4

DATABASE

Now that the field name is correct, to indicate you are finished entering the field name,

Press: ⟨←Enter⟩

The highlight skips to the Type column and waits for input. In this column you define the **field type** or the type of data a field can contain. Again the status bar provides brief instructions about how to proceed. To display a list of field types,

The ⬦ drop-down button appears to the right of a drop-down list box.

Click: ⬦ Drop-Down
or
Press: ⟨Alt⟩ + ⟨↓⟩

The drop-down list displays the eight field types. A description of the field types is presented below:

Character	Contains letters, numbers, special symbols (like %, &, #, and =), or any other printable character, including spaces.
Numeric	Contains numbers up to 20 digits including the decimal point and minus sign. Numeric fields are best used when you want to perform calculations on the values in the field.
Memo	Contains text that is variable in length and usually too long to be stored in a character field.
Logical	Accepts true, false, yes, and no values.
Date	Contains any valid date from January 1, 100, to December 31, 9999. dBASE correctly handles leap years and checks that all dates that are entered are valid dates.
Float	Used to store very large or very small numbers needed in scientific calculations.
OLE	Contains objects inserted in the table from other Windows applications that support Object Linking and Embedding.
Binary	Contains data stored in a binary format, such as image or sound data.

The employee number field will contain a four-digit number. However, unless a number is to be used in calculations, it should be assigned a Character field type. This way other characters, such as the parentheses or hyphens in a telephone number, can be included in the entry. Additionally, by specifying the type as Character, any leading zeros (for example in the zip code 07739) will be preserved, whereas leading zeros in a Numeric field type are dropped (which would make this zip code incorrectly 7739). To accept the default selection of character,

Press: ⟨←Enter⟩

The highlight moves to the Width column. The Width column is used to define the **field width**, or the maximum number of characters you can enter in the field. A character field can be from 1 to 254 characters wide. The width you make the field is determined by the largest entry that the field would be required to hold. If you make the width too small, you cannot enter all the required information. At the same time, if you make the width excessively large, it will take up unnecessary space.

You would like the EMP_NUM field to be only large enough for the four digits. To enter the field's width,

The default field width is 10 characters.

Type: 4
Press: ⏎Enter

You can click the ▣ buttons to increase or decrease the width of the field.

The highlight skips the Decimal column and moves to the Index column. The Decimal column is skipped because the field type is not numeric. The Index column is used to specify the indexed fields in the table. When a field is defined as an **index field** or **key field**, the records in the table are displayed in sorted order based on the information in that field. This makes it faster for dBASE to locate records in the table and to process other operations. A table that contains an index field is called an **indexed table**. You will learn more about indexed fields in the next lab.

To leave the Index column setting for this field at the default setting of None and move to a second field row,

Press: ⏎Enter

Your screen should be similar to Figure 1-5.

field type   field width   index setting

FIGURE 1-5

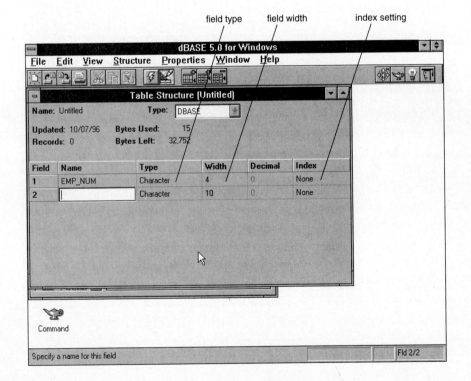

DATABASE

A second field line is displayed, indicating that dBASE is ready for input of the field name for the second field, DATE_HIRED. The field column automatically displays 2 to show this is the second field. The status bar displays "Fld 2/2." To enter the second field name,

> The field name can be typed in lowercase.

Type: **DATE_HIRED**
Press: [Tab ⇥]

Pressing [Tab ⇥] has the same effect as pressing [←Enter]: it moves the highlight to the next column to the right.

> [⇧ Shift] + [Tab ⇥] moves the highlight to the left one column.

dBASE is waiting for you to define the field type. This field will display the date the employee started working at The Sports Company in the form of month/day/year. Display the type drop-down list. The type selection that will display the date in this format is Date.

> Rather than choosing the field type from the drop-down list, you can simply type the first letter of the field type directly in the Type space or press [↑] or [↓] to cycle through all the types.

Choose: Date
Press: [Tab ⇥] or [←Enter]

dBASE skips the Width column and moves to the Index column because the Date format has a preset size of eight characters. The Width column automatically displays 8. You do not want to make the DATE_HIRED field an index field. To move to the next field line,

Press: [←Enter] or [Tab ⇥]

Your screen should be similar to Figure 1-6.

FIGURE 1-6

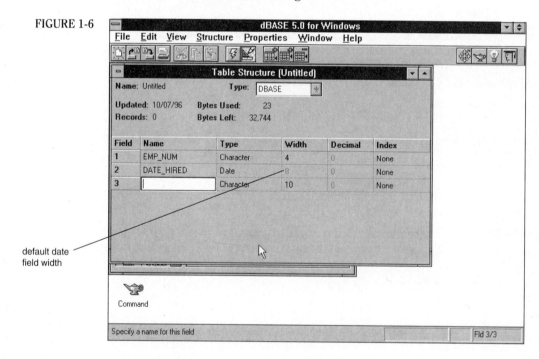

default date field width

You are ready to enter the third field. This field will hold the employee's last name. To specify the name of the third field,

Type: **LAST_NAME**
Press: [←Enter] or [Tab ⇤]

To accept the default field type of Character,

Press: [←Enter] or [Tab ⇤]

You would like the width of the last name field to be 15 characters.

Type: **15**
Press: [←Enter]

To skip the Index column,

Press: [←Enter] or [Tab ⇤]

The insertion point moves to the Field Name column of the fourth field.
   Your screen should be similar to Figure 1-7.

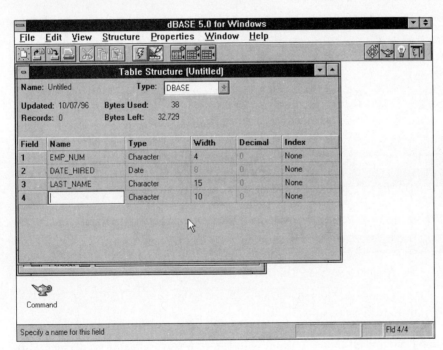

FIGURE 1-7

In the same manner, enter the information below for the next six fields. Do not be concerned if you make a mistake. You will learn how to correct errors shortly. Define the fields as follows:

Field #	Field Name	Field Type	Width	Index
4	**FIRST_NAME**	Character	**12**	None
5	**STREET**	Character	**15**	None
6	**CITY**	Character	**15**	None
7	**STATE**	Character	**2**	None
8	**ZIP_CODE**	Character	**5**	None
9	**BIRTH_DATE**	Date		None

Notice that the ZIP_CODE field type is defined as Character because it will not be used in calculations.

When you have completed the six fields, your screen should be similar to Figure 1-8.

FIGURE 1-8

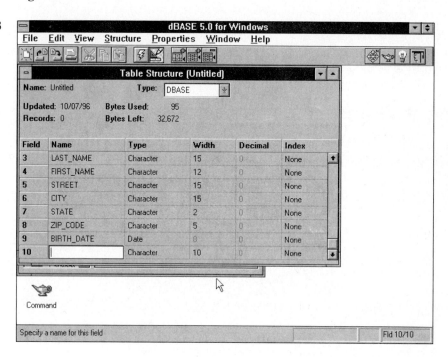

After looking over the table structure, you decide to increase the STREET field width from 15 to 20 spaces.

To move the highlight from one field to another with the mouse, point to the field and click the left mouse button. With the keyboard you can use the Tab⇆ key to move to the right one column, and ⇧Shift + Tab⇆ to move to the left one column. Move to the Width column of the STREET field and change the size to 20.

Carefully check your screen to ensure that all other field names and descriptions match those in Figure 1-8. If your screen does not match, correct it now.

Saving the Table Structure

Once you are satisfied that your field entries are correct, the table structure can be saved to the disk as a DOS file by naming it. Two commands on the File menu can be used to save a file, Save and Save As. The Save command saves the table using the same path and file name by replacing the contents of the existing file with the changes you have made. The Save As command saves the table to disk using a new file name. When you save a table for the first time, either command can be used.

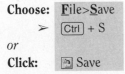

The ⊞ Save button on the SpeedBar is the same as the File>Save command.

Choose: File>Save
➤ Ctrl + S
or
Click: ⊞ Save

Your screen should be similar to Figure 1-9.

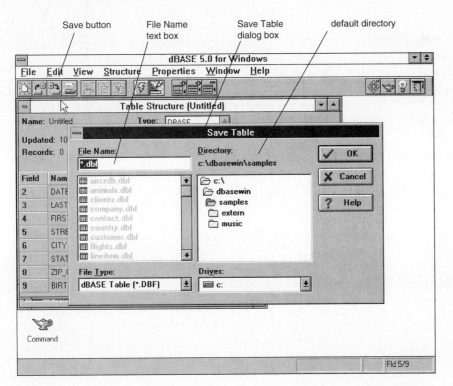

FIGURE 1-9

The Save Table dialog box is displayed. The File Name text box is selected. A table name uses the same rules as a DOS file name. It can be a maximum of eight characters and cannot contain blanks or punctuation marks other than an under-score. The table name also contains a file extension, .dbf, that is automatically added to the file name by dBASE.

The file name can be entered in either uppercase or lowercase letters. The contents of the File Name text box are highlighted, indicating that it is selected. As soon as you type, the contents will be replaced by your entry. To give the table a name that is descriptive of the contents,

Type: employee

The default directory path is displayed in the line above the Directory list box. This is most likely the drive and path containing your dBASE program files. You need to change it to the drive containing your data disk.

Note: The following command assumes that the default drive is A and that your data disk is in drive A. If your setup is different, substitute the appropriate drive and/or directory in the directions below.

To specify the default directory to be drive A,

Choose: Drives
Select: a:

Keyboard users: press ↓ to display the Drives drop-down list and then move to the option and press ←Enter to select it.

The Directory list reflects your drive selection. The command buttons allow you to accept (OK) or reject (Cancel) the command. You can choose these buttons as you would any other dialog box features.

Choose: OK

Press ←Enter to choose OK, or press Esc to choose Cancel.

The drive light goes on briefly, and the structure for your file is saved on the data disk in the drive you specified. As with all other files, it is a good idea to create a backup copy of the file in case it is accidently damaged or erased. The new table name is displayed in the Table Structure window title bar and in the Name text box.

Entering Data

You can have up to one billion records per file.

Now that the table structure is defined and saved, you can enter the employee data into the new table. To add records to a table,

Choose: View>Table Records
        ➤   F2

or

Click: ⚡ View Table Data

Your screen should be similar to Figure 1-10.

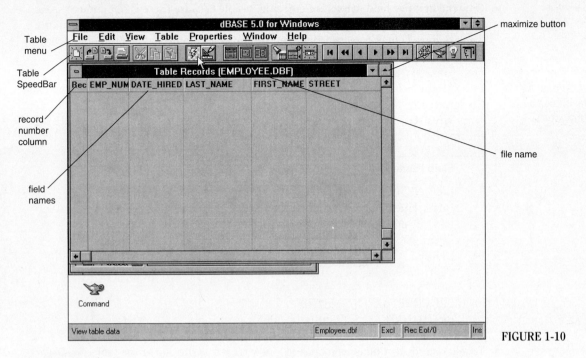

FIGURE 1-10

The Table Designer is closed and a blank Table Records window is opened. This window is used to view, add, and edit records in a table. The menu bar contains menus that can be used in the Table Records window. Likewise the SpeedBar buttons consist of buttons you can use in this window. The SpeedBar buttons are identified below.

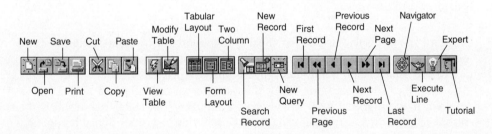

DATABASE

The field names you defined are displayed as column heads in the window. Only the first five field names are currently visible because there is not enough space across the width of the window to display all the fields. In addition, the first column displays Rec. This is a record number column that is automatically maintained by dBASE.

To display more fields, maximize the window.

All the fields are still not visible on the screen. The other fields will scroll on the screen as you enter data.

The data you enter into each field is called the **field value**. The field values for the first record are:

> Click the maximize button ▪ or choose Maximize from the Table Record control menu. ((Alt) + -).

Field Name	Field Value
EMP_NUM	1151
DATE_HIRED	October 14, 1989
LAST_NAME	Anderson
FIRST_NAME	Susan
STREET	43 South Hayden Rd.
CITY	Mesa
STATE	AZ
ZIP_CODE	84101
BIRTH_DATE	June 14, 1965

To add records to a table, you append a new record to the end of the table. Since the Employee table is empty, the first record is also the end of the table. To add records,

Choose: Table>**A**dd Records
➤ (Ctrl) + A
or
Click: ▦ Add Record

A record row is displayed. The first field is highlighted with the **selection bar** and displays an insertion point. Notice that the Rec column displays the number 1. This is a **record number** that is automatically assigned to each new record as it is entered into the table. The record number acts as an internal counter. As a new record is entered, it is assigned the next consecutive number. The status bar displays the record count as "Rec 1/1," indicating that the selection bar is positioned on the first record of a total of one record in the table.

The insertion point is in the EMP_NUM field, indicating that dBASE is ready to accept entry of the data for this field. As you type, the insertion point will move in the field to show your location in the entry. To enter the employee number for the first record,

Type: 1151

dBASE beeps and moves the selection bar to the next field, DATE_HIRED. When a field value fills the defined field width, dBASE automatically moves to the next column. The date field already contains slashes to separate the numbers in the date entry. Therefore, all you need to type are the numbers. To enter the date hired for this record (this date is intentionally incorrect),

Type: 104189

Your screen should be similar to Figure 1-11.

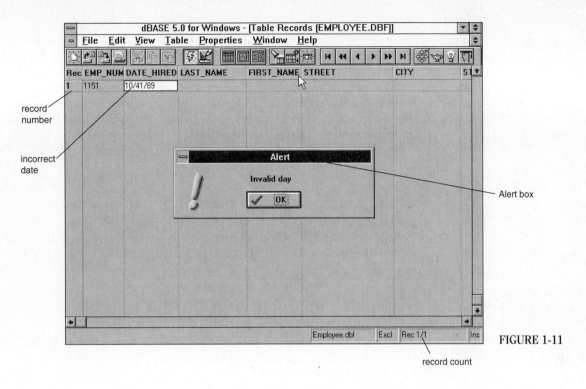

FIGURE 1-11

The Alert message "Invalid day" is displayed. dBASE automatically performs basic **checks** on the data as it is entered. A check ensures that the data that is entered into a field meets certain requirements or standards. For example, a check for a numeric field would prevent you from entering an alphabetic character as the field value. In this case, the check determined that the date entered (10/41/89) is not valid because there cannot be 41 days in a month.

To clear the message box,

Choose: OK

The insertion point moves back to the beginning of the entry. To correct the date entry,

Press: → (2 times)

The insertion point moved two spaces to the right. To replace the 41 with 14,

Type: 14

To complete the entry,

Press: ←Enter

The corrected date is accepted, and you are now ready to enter the employee's last name. The data you enter in a character field must be typed just as you want it to appear. Unlike field names, which are displayed in uppercase even if you type them in lowercase letters, the information you enter for each record is displayed just as you type it.

It is very important to be consistent when entering field values. For example, if you decide to use all uppercase characters to enter the last name field value, then every record should have the last name entered in all uppercase characters. Also, be careful not to enter a blank space before or after a field entry. This can cause problems when using the table to locate information. If data is entered in a consistent manner, it is easier to locate information and to create accurate reports from the data in the table.

Enter the last name data exactly as shown below:

Type: Anderson
Press: ←Enter

Because the field value does not fill the field, you must press ←Enter to move to the next field column. You can also use the Tab⇆ key to enter the data and move to the next field. To enter the first name using this feature,

Type: Susan
Press: Tab⇆

The first name field was entered and the selection bar moved to the next field, STREET.

To enter the address,

Type: 43 South Hayden Rd.

You decide to change the address by abbreviating South. The → or ← keys will move the insertion point within the entry. With the mouse, you can click on the location in the entry to move the insertion point. The mouse pointer is an I-beam to help you place the insertion point.

Press: ← (11 times)
or
Click: to the right of the "h" in "South"

To abbreviate South as "S.",

Press: Backspace (4 times)
Type: .

To complete the entry,

Press: ←Enter

Enter the field values for the remaining fields, typing the information exactly as it appears below. The fields will scroll on the screen as you move to the right. If you make typing errors, use the [Backspace] key to delete the error and then type the entry correctly.

Field Name	Field Value
CITY	**Mesa**
STATE	**AZ**
ZIP_CODE	**84101**
BIRTH_DATE	**061465**

☞
Remember to press [←Enter] or [Tab ⇥] to move to the next field if the field value does not fill the field width.

Your screen should be similar to Figure 1-12.

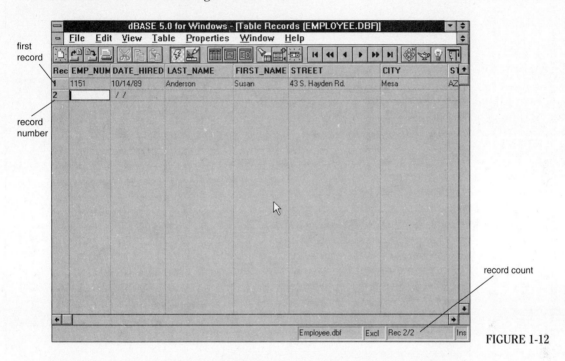

FIGURE 1-12

The data for the first record is now complete. The selection bar has moved to the first field on the next row and waits for you to enter the employee number for the second record. The status indicator displays "Rec 2/2." As soon as you move to another record, the data is saved on the disk.

Enter the following data into the second record.

Field Name	Field Value
EMP_NUM	**0434**
DATE_HIRED	**100490**
LAST_NAME	**Long**
FIRST_NAME	**William**
STREET	**947 S. Forest St.**
CITY	**Tempe**
STATE	**AZ**
ZIP_CODE	**86301**
BIRTH_DATE	**042070**

DATABASE

Your screen should be similar to Figure 1-13.

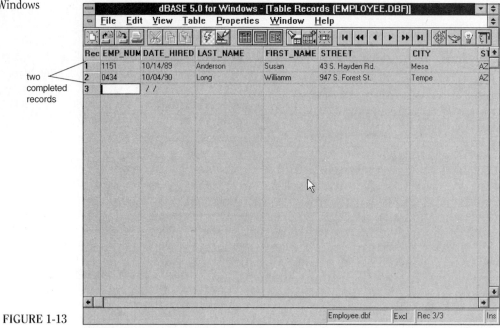

two
completed
records

FIGURE 1-13

When you have completed entering the data for the second record, dBASE is ready for you to enter the data for the third record. The second record was automatically assigned the record number 2.

Although you have entered two records, you can see only the first six columns of each record. The Table menu contains commands that can be used to move from record to record in the Table Record window. However, the same actions can be performed more quickly using the shortcut keys or SpeedBar buttons presented below.

Menu	Key	SpeedBar	Moves to
Table>Previous Record	↑	◄	Previous record
Table>Next Record	↓	►	Next record
Table>Previous Page	Page Up	◄◄	Previous screenful of records
Table>Next Page	Page Down	►►	Next screenful of records
Table>Top Record	Ctrl + Page Up	I◄	First record
Table>Bottom Record	Ctrl + Page Down	►I	Last record

To move to the first record,

Press: ⬆ (2 times) or Ctrl + Page Up
or
Click: ◄ (2 times) or ◄◄

The selection bar is on the same field of the first record. When a record contains the selection bar, the record is the **current record**, or the record that will be affected by your next action. The field is the **current field**. Then to move field by field to the right,

Press: Tab↹ (8 times)

You moved through all the fields of the first record and are positioned on the last field of the first record. The record number column remains stationary in the window, while all other fields have scrolled to the left. Notice that when you move to a field that already contains an entry, the field value is highlighted and the insertion point is positioned at the end of the entry. This indicates that the entire entry is selected and will be replaced as soon as you type a character. Moving the insertion point will clear the highlight and allow you to correct, or edit, part of the entry. To see this,

Press: ←

The highlight is cleared. Now you could edit the field value if needed. To move quickly back to the first field of this record,

Press: Ctrl + Home

With the mouse, you can click directly on a field to move the selection bar to it. You can also use the scroll bars to move the table image in the window either horizontally or vertically to bring into view records and fields that are not currently visible.

Use the horizontal scroll bar to scroll the table image horizontally until the BIRTH_DATE field is visible.

Click on the BIRTH_DATE field of record 2.

Notice that the entry in the field is not highlighted as it is when you move to a field using the keys or SpeedBar buttons. The entry can be highlighted by dragging the mouse over the entry.

Scroll the table image back to display the EMP_NUM column and move to the EMP_NUM field of record 1.

Viewing Records

Scrolling the window is sometimes a cumbersome way to view the data in the table. To make it easier to view data, dBASE allows you to change how data is displayed in a table. There are three table window layouts:

Browse layout	The current layout, which displays many records at the same time, with one record per row
Form layout	Displays a single record in a table by arranging the fields horizontally with field names above values
Columnar layout	Displays a single record in a table by arranging the fields in two columns, with field names on the left and values on the right

To view the records in Form layout,

Choose: View>Form Layout

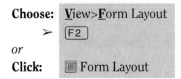

or

Click: ▦ Form Layout

Your screen should be similar to Figure 1-14.

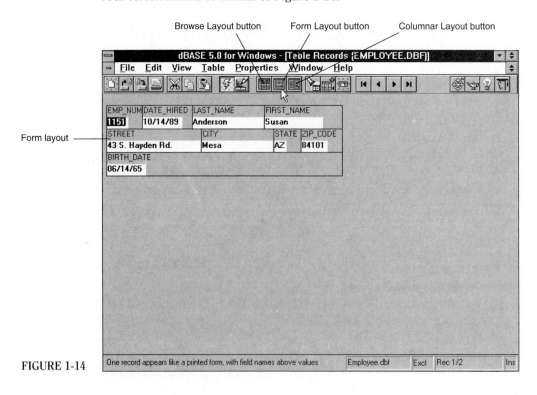

FIGURE 1-14

The records are displayed as a printed form with the field names above the values. The record that was the current record in Browse layout is the record that is displayed in Form layout. To display the record in Columnar layout,

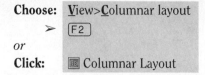

Choose: View>Columnar layout
  ➢ F2

or

Click: ▦ Columnar Layout

The F2 function key cycles through the layouts.

The Columnar layout displays a single record at a time with field names in the left column and field values in the right column. Now you can see many more fields of data at once in the window for each record. In both Form and Columnar layout, the displayed record is the current record. To navigate in Columnar layout, refer to the following chart.

Moves	Key	SpeedBar	Table Command
Down one field	↵Enter, Tab↹, ↓	◂	
Up one field	⇧Shift + ↵Enter or Tab↹, ↑	▸	
Previous Record	Page Up	◂◂	Previous record
Next Record	Page Down	▸▸	Next record
First Record	Ctrl + Page Up	◂◂|	Top record
Last Record	Ctrl + Page Down	|▸▸	Bottom record

Move to record 2.
The employee information for William Long, record number 2, is displayed.
Check both records for accuracy and edit them as necessary.
  Now that you have looked at the first two records, you want to continue adding more records to the Employee table. You can add and edit records in Columnar or Form layout just as you did in Browse layout. To add another record,

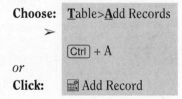

Choose: Table>Add Records
  ➢
    Ctrl + A
or
Click: ▦ Add Record

A blank record is displayed and "Rec 3/3" is displayed in the status bar.

Enter the following data for the third record.

Field Name	Field Value
EMP_NUM	0234
HIRE_DATE	111289
LAST_NAME	Bergstrom
FIRST_NAME	Drew
STREET	843 W. Southern Ave.
CITY	Mesa
STATE	AZ
ZIP_CODE	84101
BIRTH_DATE	080761

When you entered the employee's birth date (last field in the record), the insertion point moved to the EMP_NUM field of the next blank entry form.

Finally, you would like to enter several more records into the table. Enter the data for the following two records into the table as records 4 and 5.

Field Name	Record 4	Record 5
EMP_NUM	0728	0839
HIRE_DATE	011591	031491
LAST_NAME	Toroyan	Artis
FIRST_NAME	Lucy	Jose
STREET	2348 S. Bala Dr.	358 Maple Dr.
CITY	Tempe	Scottsdale
STATE	AZ	AZ
ZIP_CODE	85301	85205
BIRTH_DATE	031561	121063

Enter a final record as record 6 using your first and last names. Enter 9999 as your employee number and the current date in the DATE_HIRED field. The information you enter in all the other fields can be fictitious. Do not press ←Enter after entering your date of birth.

Your screen should be similar to Figure 1-15.

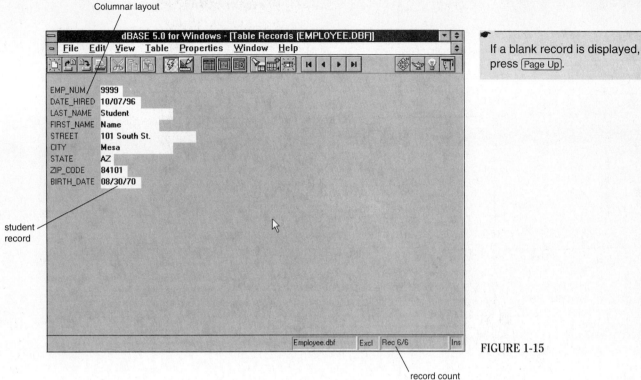

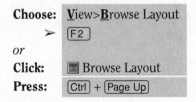

FIGURE 1-15

If a blank record is displayed, press Page Up.

The record count in the status bar shows that there are a total of six records in the table.

To quickly switch back to Browse layout to see the records you just entered in the table,

Choose: View>Browse Layout
  ➢ F2
or
Click: 🔲 Browse Layout
Press: Ctrl + Page Up

DATABASE

Your screen should be similar to Figure 1-16.

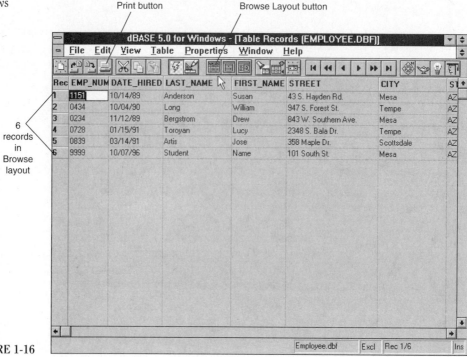

FIGURE 1-16

The six records are displayed.

Check each of the records and edit any entries that are incorrect.

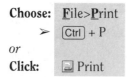

Use the scroll bars or the navigation keys to scroll through the records.

Printing a Table

You have finished for the day and you would like to print a copy of the records in this table. The Print command on the File menu generates a printout of the records in the table.

Note: See your instructor about directions for using your printer.

Choose: File>Print

➤ Ctrl + P

or

Click: 🖨 Print

The Print Records dialog box is displayed. The default print settings print one copy of all the records in the table. Records are printed in the current layout of the Table Records window.

In Browse layout, when a record is wider than can be printed across the width of the page, dBASE prints the additional data on the next page.

To print the table,

Choose: OK

The Printing message box is displayed. After a few moments, the records are printed. The six records are displayed using the default printout format. This format automatically displays the file name at the top of the report as a header. The field names are displayed above each column and a page number is centered as a footer at the bottom of each page. The Record number column is not printed. The contents of each record wrap to a second page because the record length is too long to fit across the width of the page on one line. This makes reading a listing of records difficult. Later labs will demonstrate the other print features of dBASE.

Exiting dBASE

You will continue to build and use the table of employee records in the next lab. Because dBASE saves the records as they were entered into the table, you do not need to save the table before exiting dBASE.

There are several ways you can exit the dBASE program. You can choose the Exit command on the File menu, double-click on the application window control-menu box, choose Close from the control menu, or press Alt + F4 .

Using any of these methods, exit dBASE.

Note: You will receive an error message if you remove the data disk before the dBASE program has been completely exited. This can cause problems with the tables and the data entered in them.

Always use one of these commands when ending a dBASE session. If you end the session by resetting your computer without following this procedure, you may damage the open tables. This could cause loss of data.

Key Terms

menu bar   (DB9)
SpeedBar   (DB9)
status bar   (DB9)
mode   (DB9)
desktop   (DB9)
Navigator   (DB9)
Command window   (DB9)
user interface   (DB9)
database   (DB9)
table   (DB9)
record   (DB9)
field   (DB9)
relational database   (DB9)

relation   (DB9)
structure   (DB12)
field type   (DB16)
field width   (DB17)
index field   (DB17)
key field   (DB17)
indexed table   (DB17)
field value   (DB24)
selection bar   (DB24)
record number   (DB24)
checks   (DB25)
current record   (DB29)
current field   (DB29)

Command Summary

Command	Shortcut	SpeedBar	Action
File>New		▢	Creates a new file
File>Exit	Alt + F4		Exits application
File>Save	Ctrl + S	▢	Saves table structure using same path and file name
File>Save As			Saves table structure using a new file name
View>Table Records	F2	▢	View used to view, add, and edit records in a table
Table>Add Records	Ctrl + A	▢	Adds record to table
Table>Previous Record	↑	◀	Moves to previous record
Table>Next Record	↓	▶	Moves to next record
Table>Previous Page	Page Up	◀◀	Moves to previous page
Table>Next Page	Page Down	▶▶	Moves to next page
Table>Top Record	Ctrl + Page Up	◀◀	Moves to first record
Table>Bottom Record	Ctrl + Page Down	▶▶	Moves to last record
View>Form Layout	F2	▢	Displays a single record as a printed form with field names displayed above field values
View>Columnar Layout	F2	▢	Displays a single record at a time with field names in left column and values in right
View>Browse Layout	F2	▢	Displays multiple records
File>Print	Ctrl + P	▢	Prints file

LAB REVIEW

Matching

1. relation _____ a. displays information about tasks and current state of operation
2. database _____ b. where the information in a database is stored
3. status bar _____ c. collection of related information
4. table _____ d. the current record is record 1 of four records
5. record _____ e. accesses Help system
6. SpeedBar _____ f. collection of related fields
7. field _____ g. a link between two tables based on a common field
8. Rec 1/4 _____ h. area where windows are displayed
9. F1 _____ i. collection of related characters
10. desktop _____ j. contains icons that represent shortcut buttons for common menu commands

Fill-In Questions

1. Identify the parts of the dBASE screen by entering the appropriate term on the lines below.

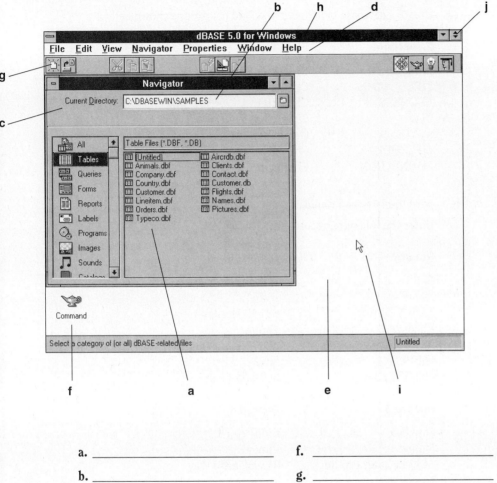

a. _____   f. _____

b. _____   g. _____

c. _____   h. _____

d. _____   i. _____

e. _____   j. _____

Practice Exercises

1. Audra Weiss is about to move to another city. She wants to gather information about her friends and relatives that she is leaving. To best organize this information, she wants to create a database using dBASE.

    a. Create a database table using the field definitions shown below.

Field Name	Field Type	Field Width	Index
LAST_NAME	Character	15	None
FIRST_NAME	Character	10	None
ADDRESS	Character	22	None
CITY	Character	15	None
STATE	Character	2	None
ZIP_CODE	Character	5	None
PHONE_NUM	Character	12	None

    b. Save the table as Friends.

    c. Enter the following records into the table.

Record 1	Record 2
Bell	Lindstrom
Jason	Ryan
1546 N. Tatum	821 N. Heritage
Phoenix	Tempe
AZ	AZ
85049	85222
602-555-2349	602-555-6945

Record 3	Record 4
Sanchez	Elder
Miguel	Pliney
1449 E. Southern Rd.	641 Historic Way
Mesa	Tucson
AZ	AZ
85629	85004
602-555-1051	602-555-6462

    d. Enter your name in the appropriate field of record 5. All other fields can be fictitious.

    e. Print the table.

You will use this table in Practice Exercise 1 of Lab 2.

2. Pam is the manager of Travel Abroad, a small travel agency specializing in group tours. One of Pam's responsibilities is to maintain employee records. To help her with this job, she wants to create a database of the employee records using dBASE.

    a. Create a database table using the field definitions shown below.

Field Name	Field Type	Field Width	Index
EMP_NUM	Character	3	None
LAST_NAME	Character	15	None
FIRST_NAME	Character	10	None
MID_INT	Character	1	None
ADDRESS	Character	45	None
DATE_HIRED	Date		None

    b. Save the table as Staff.

    c. Enter the following records into the table.

Record 1

234
[Your last name]
[Your first name]
[Your middle initial]
34 Maple Dr., San Jose, CA 95192
[Current date]

Record 2

245
Masters
Kevin
W
85 Ash Ave., Danville, CA 92401
September 5, 1994

Record 3

342
Johnson
William
J
3456 Pine St., Santa Ana, CA 92706
October 6, 1994

Record 4

311
O'Hearn
Paul
J
984 Mountain Dr., San Diego, CA 92182
May 18, 1994

    d.   Print the table.

You will use this table in Practice Exercise 1 of Lab 3.

3.   Lois works at an auto parts warehouse. Her supervisor has asked her to create a database table to keep track of the inventory.

    a.   Create a database table that includes the following fields.

Field	Field Type	Field Width	Index
ITEM_NUM	Character	5	None
ITEM_NAME	Character	20	None
QUANTITY	Numeric	3 (0 decimal)	None
COST	Float	5 (2 decimal)	None
SALE_PRICE	Float	5 (2 decimal)	None

    b.   Save the table as Autoinv.

    c.   Enter the following records.

Record 1

89333
Air Filter
25
15.00
20.00

Record 2

34567
Gas Cap
35
5.00
9.00

Record 3

43243
Gas Filter
42
3.00
5.50

Record 4

21294
Distributor Cap
89
13.50
20.00

Record 5

33738
Plug Wire
13
2.00
4.50

Record 6

83922
Spark Plugs
35
1.80
3.50

    d.   Enter your name in the ITEM_NAME field of record 7. Leave all the other fields blank.

    e.   Print the table.

4.   Peter owns a consignment furniture store, New to You. He currently keeps his consignees and payment records in a small accounting ledger. His business has grown considerably since he started it a year ago, so he has decided to invest in a computer. He wants to keep track of his consignees and payments using dBASE.

a.   Create a database table using the field information defined below.

Field Name	Field Type	Field Width	Index
NUMBER	Character	5	None
LAST_NAME	Character	12	None
FIRST_NAME	Character	10	None
ADDRESS	Character	20	None
CITY	Character	10	None
STATE	Character	2	None
ZIP_CODE	Character	5	None
PHONE	Character	8	None

b.   Save the table as Consign.

c.   Enter the following records into the table.

Record 1	Record 2
67245	64656
Tyler	Theiler
Sean	Jeff
432 W. Maple Ave.	843 E. Pine St.
San Jose	San Jose
CA	CA
94822	94821
893-4854	543-0943

d.   Enter a third record in the table using your name in the first and last name fields. Your consignment number is 23952. The address and phone can be fictitious.

e.   Print the table.

f.   Create a second database table using the field information defined below.

Field Name	Field Type	Field Width	Index
ITEM_NUM	Character	3	None
CONSG_NUM	Character	5	None
ITEM_NAME	Character	25	None
PRICE	Float	6 (2 decimal)	None
PERCENTAGE	Numeric	3 (0 decimal)	None

g.   Save the table as Furnish.

h. Enter the following records into the table.

Record 1	Record 2
783	432
67245	64656
Sofa	Coffee Table
800.00	85.00
25	15

Record 3	Record 4
395	783
67245	23952
Queen Bed	Chair
350.00	450.00
20	20

Record 5	Record 6
432	386
64656	23952
End Table	Dresser
45.00	150.00
15	20

i. Print the table.

You will use this table in Practice Exercise 3 in Lab 3.

5. Michael owns a carpet business that specializes in carpeting for custom homes. The business is growing and Michael has decided to buy a computer to help him keep track of his clients, employees, and inventory.

   a. Create a database table to help Michael keep track of his clients. The table should include each client's name, address, telephone number, and type of job. Use field names of your choice. Be sure to include one field that uniquely identifies the client. Save the table using a name of your choice.

   b. Enter your name and appropriate information as the first record.

   c. Enter eight additional records to the table using either real or fictitious data.

   d. Print the data.

6. Karen is a third-year student at a midwestern university. She would like to create a database table of all the classes she has taken to date. Create a table that contains the information you feel would be appropriate for this table, for example, class number, course title, credit hours, and grade. Enter at least 10 records using either real or fictitious data. Enter your name as one of the class records. Print the table.

Working with Tables and Designing a Custom Form

2

CASE STUDY

You have continued to work on your database of employee records by adding more records to the table. You have noticed several errors in the records you entered that need to be corrected. You also realize that you forgot to include a field for the employee's sex in the table. Moreover, you would like to create a customized form to make adding records to the table easier.

Using the Navigator

Load Windows. Put your data disk in drive A (or the appropriate drive for your system). Load dBASE for Windows.

Competencies

After completing this lab, you will know how to:

1. Use the Navigator.
2. Edit and delete records.
3. Locate information in a table.
4. Restructure a table.
5. Freeze a field.
6. Sort records.
7. Index a table.
8. Create a customized form.
9. Select and move objects.
10. Enhance a form.
11. Enter data in a custom form.

DATABASE

Your screen should be similar to Figure 2-1.

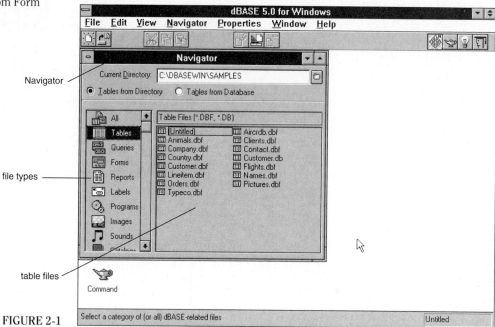

Navigator

file types

table files

FIGURE 2-1

The Navigator window is used to create and use different types of dBASE files. The left side of the Navigator window displays a list of file types. The most common type of file used in dBASE is a table. For this reason, Tables is the selected option. You will learn about the other types of files, such as reports and forms, later in the labs.

The file list on the right side of the window displays the names of all files associated with the selected file type. In this case, table files in the current directory are listed. The Current Directory text box displays the drive and path that dBASE is accessing. Most likely this is the drive and path containing your dBASE program files. If this is the case, you need to change it to the drive containing your data disk.

Note: The following procedure assumes the default drive is not A and that your data disk is in drive A. If your setup is different, substitute the appropriate drive and/or directory in the following directions.

To specify drive A,

Use ⎡Tab⮀⎤ to move within the
Navigator window or click on
the area with the mouse.

Choose: Current **D**irectory

If necessary, select the text in the Current Directory text box.

Type: **A:** (or the appropriate drive for your system)
Press: ⎡←Enter⎤

All the table files on your data disk are displayed in the Table Files list box. The table with the additional employee records in it is Employ2. To open the Employ2 table,

Select: Employ2.dbf
Choose: File>Open
       ➢   Ctrl + O
or
Click: 📄 Open
Choose: OK

The Table Records window is open and displays the first nine records in the table in Browse layout.

To view more records, maximize the Table Records window.
Your screen should be similar to Figure 2-2.

FIGURE 2-2

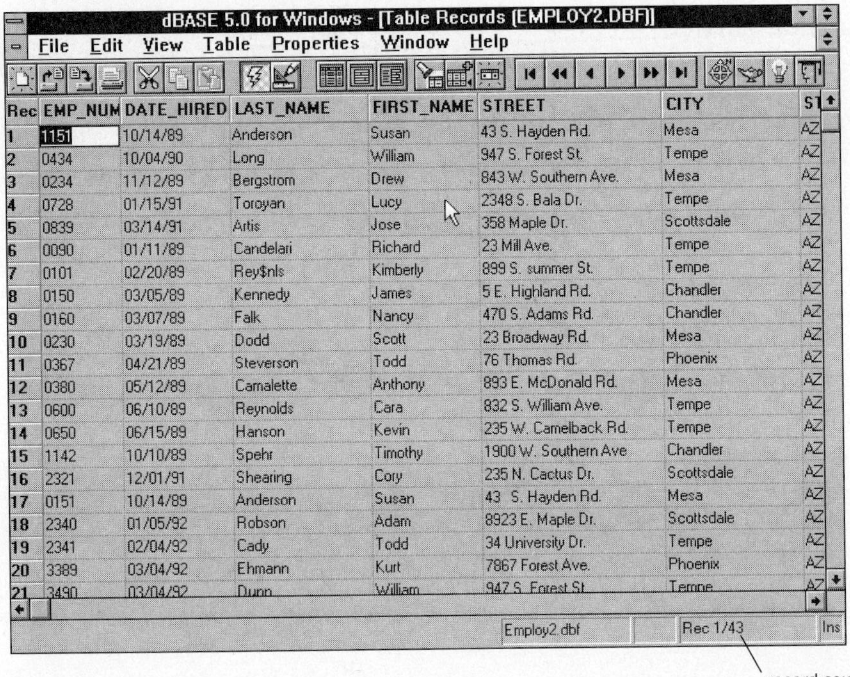

record count

The table now displays the first 20 records. The status bar record count indicates that there are 43 records in the table.

As you learned in Lab 1, you can use the commands on the Table menu, the command shortcut keys, and the following navigation keys and SpeedBar buttons to move through a table of records:

Move to	Table Menu	Shortcut Key	SpeedBar
First record, same field	Top Record	Ctrl + Page Up	◄
Last record, same field	Bottom Record	Ctrl + Page Down	►
Next record	Next Record	↓	►
Previous record	Previous Record	↑	◄
Next page of records	Next Page	Page Down	►►
Previous page of records	Previous Page	Page Up	◄◄
Next field		Tab↹ or ←Enter	
Previous field		⇧Shift + Tab↹	
Last field of record		Ctrl + End	
First field of record		Ctrl + Home	

Generally it is quickest to use the navigation keys, shortcut keys, or SpeedBar buttons. If you have a mouse, you can also use the scroll bars to navigate through the records in the table and then click on the field.

To move down a page of records on the screen,

Click: ►► Next Page
or
Press: Page Down

Records 20 through 39 are displayed. The last record on the previous screenful of records is the first record on this screen.

To display the remaining records in the table,

Click: ►► Next Page
or
Press: Page Down

Records 39 through 43 are displayed.

To return to the first screenful of records, you could press Page Up twice. However, to quickly move to the first record,

Click: ◄ First Record
or
Press: Ctrl + Page Up

Use the navigation keys or scroll bars to display the rest of the data. When you have finished looking at the records, return to the first field of record 1.

Editing Data

While reviewing the records, you may have noticed a few errors. For example, look at the LAST_NAME field for record 7. It should be Reynolds. The STREET field of record 7 also contains errors. You would like to correct these errors now.

Move to: LAST_NAME field of record 7

An insertion point is displayed in the field. You can now move the insertion point within the entry and edit the part of the entry that is incorrect. You can click on the location in the entry with the mouse to move the insertion point or use the navigation keys shown below.

Key	Effect
→ or ←	Moves from character to character within field
Ctrl + →	Moves to beginning of next word
Ctrl + ←	Moves to beginning of previous word
Home	Moves to beginning of field
End	Moves to end of field

To correct the last name to Reynolds,

Move to: $

Your screen should be similar to Figure 2-3.

> If you used the keyboard to move to the field, the last name is also highlighted. The highlight will clear when you move the insertion point.

> The mouse is an I-beam when positioned on the current field.

> When you move to a character, the insertion point should be on the left side of the character.

insertion point   mouse pointer

Rec	EMP_NUM	DATE_HIRED	LAST_NAME	FIRST_NAME	STREET	CITY	ST
1	1151	10/14/89	Anderson	Susan	43 S. Hayden Rd.	Mesa	AZ
2	0434	10/04/90	Long	William	947 S. Forest St.	Tempe	AZ
3	0234	11/12/89	Bergstrom	Drew	843 W. Southern Ave.	Mesa	AZ
4	0728	01/15/91	Toroyan	Lucy	2348 S. Bala Dr.	Tempe	AZ
5	0839	03/14/91	Artis	Jose	358 Maple Dr.	Scottsdale	AZ
6	0090	01/11/89	Candelari	Richard	23 Mill Ave.	Tempe	AZ
7	0101	02/20/89	Reysnls T	Kimberly	899 S. summer St.	Tempe	AZ
8	0150	03/05/89	Kennedy	James	5 E. Highland Rd.	Chandler	AZ
9	0160	03/07/89	Falk	Nancy	470 S. Adams Rd.	Chandler	AZ
10	0230	03/19/89	Dodd	Scott	23 Broadway Rd.	Mesa	AZ
11	0367	04/21/89	Steverson	Todd	76 Thomas Rd.	Phoenix	AZ
12	0380	05/12/89	Camalette	Anthony	893 E. McDonald Rd.	Mesa	AZ
13	0600	06/10/89	Reynolds	Cara	832 S. William Ave.	Tempe	AZ
14	0650	06/15/89	Hanson	Kevin	235 W. Camelback Rd.	Tempe	AZ
15	1142	10/10/89	Spehr	Timothy	1900 W. Southern Ave	Chandler	AZ
16	2321	12/01/91	Shearing	Cory	235 N. Cactus Dr.	Scottsdale	AZ
17	0151	10/14/89	Anderson	Susan	43 S. Hayden Rd.	Mesa	AZ
18	2340	01/05/92	Robson	Adam	8923 E. Maple Dr.	Scottsdale	AZ
19	2341	02/04/92	Cady	Todd	34 University Dr.	Tempe	AZ
20	3389	03/04/92	Ehmann	Kurt	7867 Forest Ave.	Phoenix	AZ
21	3490	03/04/92	Dunn	William	947 S. Forest St.	Tempe	AZ

dBASE 5.0 for Windows - [Table Records (EMPLOY2.DBF)]

File   Edit   View   Table   Properties   Window   Help

Employ2.dbf   Rec 7/43   Ins

FIGURE 2-3

DATABASE

To remove the $,

Press: Delete

The Delete key removes the character to the right of the insertion point. To enter the letter "o" following the "n,"

Press: →
Type: o

Then to insert a "d" between the "l" and "s,"

Press: →
Type: d

To complete the correction,

Press: ←Enter

Your screen should be similar to Figure 2-4.

FIGURE 2-4

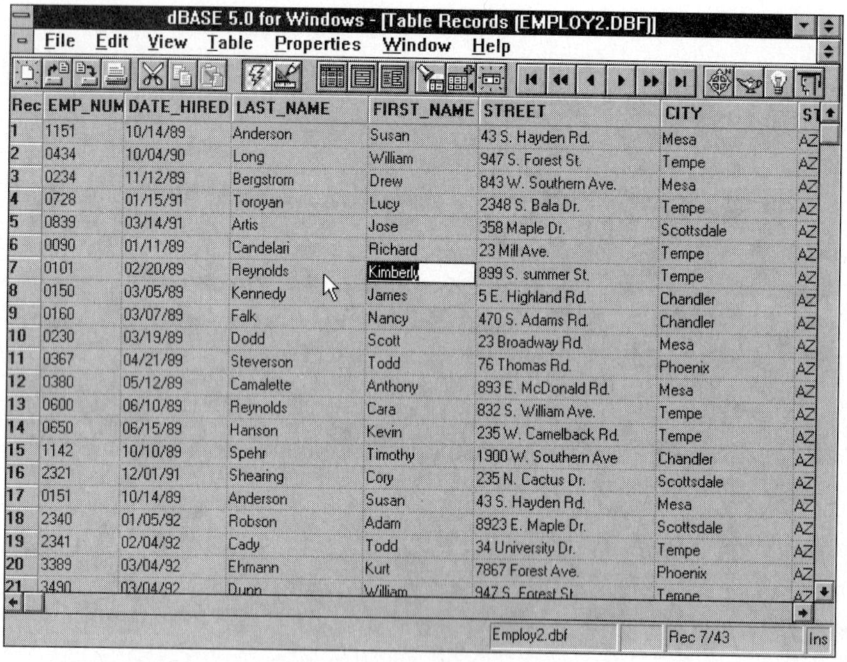

The insertion point has moved to the next field.

The STREET field for record 7 also has some typing errors. To correct the address to 8949 S. Summer St.,

Press: Tab ←→
Press: Home
Press: → (2 times)
Type: 4

To capitalize the street name,

Press: Ctrl + → (2 times)
Press: Delete
Type: S
Press: ←Enter

Now you want to check the fields to the right.

Press: Ctrl + End
Press: Page Down

Replacing Record Values

While viewing the records, you notice that some of the records, for example records 27 and 32, have lowercase letters in the STATE field. You could edit each record individually, or you can use the Replace Records command on the Table menu to quickly change multiple records.

Move to the STATE field.

The Replace Record command is also available on the SpeedMenu. The **SpeedMenu** contains commonly used commands from many different menus.

To display the SpeedMenu, click the right mouse button.

A menu of commands that are available on the Table Records menu is displayed. The SpeedMenu commands will vary depending upon the window that is open at the time.

Choose: Replace Records

Choose: Table>Replace Records
  ➤ Ctrl + R

Your screen should be similar to Figure 2-5.

Find What
text box

Replace Records
dialog box

Replace With
text box

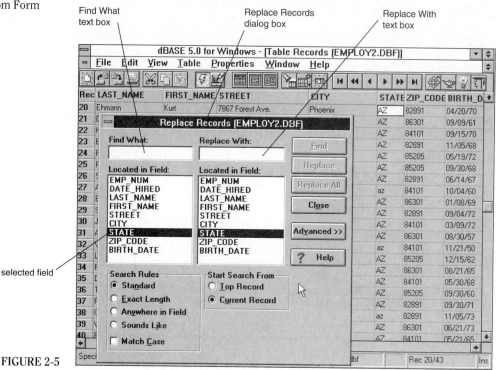

selected field

FIGURE 2-5

The Replace Records dialog box is displayed. To direct the program to find all entries with "az" in the STATE field, in the Find What text box,

Type: az
Press: Tab ↹

The insertion point moves to the Replace With text box. To change all the located values to AZ,

Type: AZ

Notice that both of the Located in Field list boxes have the STATE field highlighted. This is because this is the field that is currently selected in the database. The options under Search Rules define the search parameters. The default selection, Standard, searches for records whose field value begins with or matches the Find What value, regardless of case. To make the search case-sensitive,

Choose: Match Case

To replace all the located values of az with AZ at one time,

Choose: Replace All

The message box indicates that three records were located and asks if you want to commit your changes. To change all three records,

Choose: Yes

To close the Replace Records dialog box,

Choose: Close

The highlight is positioned on the last record in the database. To see how the Replace Record command changed the entries,

Choose: ◄◄
or
Press: Page Up

Your screen should be similar to Figure 2-6.

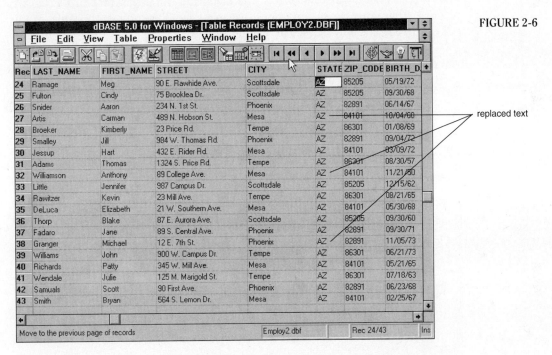

FIGURE 2-6

Look at record 27.

The value in the STATE field has been changed appropriately for this record and all other records meeting the conditions specified in the Find What text box. Using the Replace All command quickly changed all the records. Care should be used when replacing all values in a field because the changes cannot be undone.

Deleting Records

Move to the EMP_NUM field of the first record.

As you look over the table to locate any other errors, you notice that records 1 and 17 have identical information in all fields except for the employee numbers. You think the same record was entered twice with different employee numbers. By checking the employee card, you determined that record 17 is correct and you want to remove record 1.

Deleting records involves a two-step process. First you mark the record for deletion. Then you **pack** the file to permanently remove the marked record from the table. You mark a record for deletion using the Delete Selected Record command on the Table menu. The shortcut for this command is Ctrl + U.

To mark record 1,

This command is also on the SpeedMenu.

Choose: **T**able>**D**elete Selected Record
➢   Ctrl + U

The record is no longer displayed in the table, and the first record in the table is record 2. The status bar still indicates that there are 43 records in the table. At this point, the record is only marked for deletion.

If you accidentally mark a record for deletion, it can be unmarked. To try this, you will mark record 2 for deletion and then unmark it.

Mark record 2 for deletion.

To unmark a record for deletion, you must be able to see the record. To see the records marked for deletion,

Choose: **P**roperties>**D**esktop

Your screen should be similar to Figure 2-7.

Your screen may display different information in the dialog box.

FIGURE 2-7

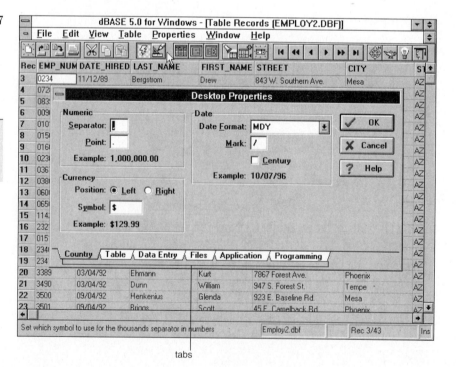

tabs

The Desktop Properties dialog box is displayed. This dialog box is a tab dialog box. A **tab dialog box** displays tabs across the bottom of the dialog box that are used to access different folders of related options. The highlighted tab indicates the folder that is open. The tab folder that contains the setting to exclude marked records is in the Table folder. If this folder is not already open, to open it,

Choose: Table

The Table tab folder is displayed. The option that excludes marked records from the table is Deleted. By default, the Deleted option is checked. When checked, you do not see deleted records in the Table Records window. To display the records marked for deletion in the table, the Deleted option must be unchecked. To do this,

Choose: Dele_t_ed>OK

A Delete column ("Del") is displayed after the record number column in the table.

Move to: Record 1

Notice that the first two records display an X in the Delete column, indicating they are marked for deletion.
   To unmark the second record,

Choose: **T**able>**T**able Utilities>**R**ecall Records

The Recall Records dialog box is displayed. This dialog box allows you to recall all the marked records or specific marked records. You would like to recall the second record. To do this,

Choose: Recor_d_

To recall record 2, in the Record text box,

Type: 2
Choose: OK

The X is removed from the Del column for record 2. Record 1 is still marked.
   You have completed the first step in removing a record from a database file by marking it for deletion. The record remains part of the file until completion of the second step, permanently removing the record from the table by packing the table. Multiple records can be marked individually for deletion; however, as soon as you use the command to delete the marked records, all marked records are deleted immediately. To actually delete the marked record,

Choose: **T**able>**T**able Utilities>**P**ack Records

A dialog box appears advising you that the file must be in exclusive use to continue. Exclusive use stops another user from using the same file, which is possible on a network. By default, exclusive use is off. However, when certain actions are performed that structurally change the file, such as deleting a record or field, exclusive use is required.

> To open a folder, click on the tab or use the [Tab ⇆] or [⇧ Shift] + [Tab ⇆] key to move to the tab area, and then press [→] or [←] to move to the folder of your choice.

> To quickly mark or unmark a record, you can click on the Delete column of the record.

DATABASE

To reopen the file exclusively,

Choose: Yes

Your screen should be similar to Figure 2-8.

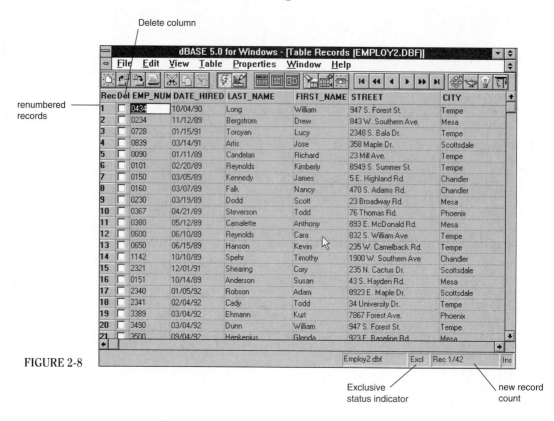

FIGURE 2-8

"Excl" appears in the status bar to show that you have exclusive use of the file. The file will remain in exclusive use throughout the rest of the session.

The file on disk is accessed and the marked record is permanently removed. All records are renumbered to maintain the internal count of records in the table. The status bar reflects the fact that there are now 42 records in the table.

Be careful when you pack a table, because any records that are deleted cannot be recovered. The only way to get them back is to enter them again.

To turn off the display of the Del column in the table,

Choose: Properties>Desktop>Deleted>OK

Locating Information in a Table

Part of your job is to update employee records. Over the past few days, you have received several change forms to update the employee records. The first change request is for Carman Artis, who recently married and has both a name and an address change.

To locate this record, you could look through all the last names until you found Artis. If the table was small, this method would be acceptable. For large tables, however, this method would be time consuming. A more efficient way to find specific values in records is to use the Find Records command on the Table menu.

Choose: T̲able>F̲ind Records
   ➢   Ctrl + F
or
Click: 🔍 Find Records

Find Records is also on the SpeedMenu.

Your screen should be similar to Figure 2-9.

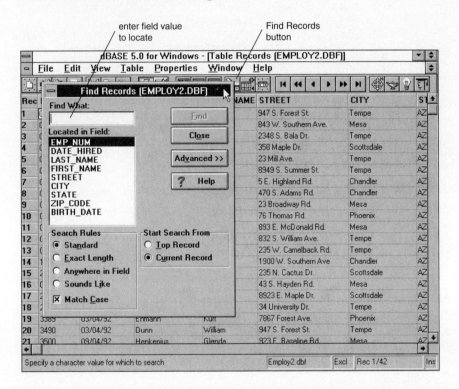

enter field value to locate

Find Records button

FIGURE 2-9

The Find Records dialog box is displayed. In the Find What text box you enter the field value you want to locate. The value can be any combination of characters and spaces, in this case, Artis. dBASE uses this value to locate an exact match in the database table.

Type: Artis

Next you need to choose from the Located in Field list box the field in which the value is to be found.

If you are using the keyboard, press Tab ⇥ to move to the list of field names.

Select: LAST_NAME

The other options in this dialog box allow you to specify how the search is performed. Notice that these options are the same as those in the Replace Records dialog box. The Match Case option is selected because you selected it in the Replace

DATABASE

Records dialog box. The Start Search From options specify where dBASE starts the search. By default, Current Record is selected. Both these settings are acceptable.

Choose: Find

If the Find Records dialog box covers the LAST_NAME field, move it to a new location in the window.

Your screen should be similar to Figure 2-10.

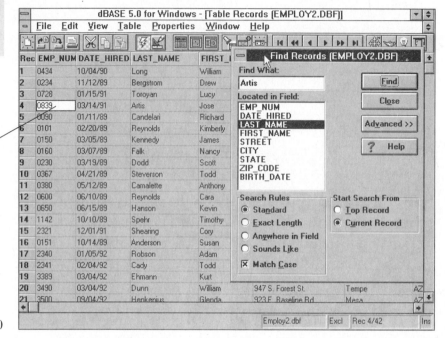

located record

FIGURE 2-10

dBASE searches the table and moves to the first occurrence of the Find What value. The highlight is positioned on record number 4.

Note: If your command did not locate this record, reissue the command and make sure you enter the name Artis exactly as shown, and that you are searching the LAST_NAME field.

To close the Find Records dialog box,

Choose: Close

You can now change the last name to Richards.
If necessary, move to the LAST_NAME field and highlight the field value.

If you used the mouse to move to the field, double-click the entry to highlight the entire contents.

Type: **Richards**

After typing the name, you notice that this is the record for Jose, not Carman. You have changed the wrong record. Since you have not yet moved to the next field, you can use the Undo command on the Edit menu to undo changes made to the field value.

To quickly undo the change made to this record,

Choose: Edit>Undo
> ➢   Ctrl + Z

The last name returns to Artis. You can use Undo to cancel your last action as long as you do not move off the field. Once you move off the field, the change is saved to disk and cannot be undone.

To continue the search to locate the next record with the last name Artis,

Choose: Table>Find Records
> ➢   Ctrl + F

or

Click: 🔍 Find Records

Enter Artis in the Find What text box and if necessary, select the LAST_NAME field from the Located in Field list box.

To locate the next record for Artis,

Choose: Find

After a moment the highlight is positioned on record number 26. This is Carman Artis's record.

Close the Find Records dialog box. Change the last name to Richards and the address to 5401 E. Thomas Rd.

The other three changes you need to make are listed below. Search the table for the following records and correct the entries.

Name	Field(s)	Correction
Adam Robson	STREET	**4290 E. Alameda Dr.**
Kevin Hanson	CITY, ZIP_CODE	**Scottsdale, 85205**
Meg Ramage	LAST_NAME	**Miller**

> Choose Find again if dBASE stayed on record 4. Make sure you entered the name Artis exactly as shown, and that you are searching the LAST_NAME field.

> Use the Start Search From Top Record option to begin from the first record.

Restructuring a Table

While looking over the table, you notice that you forgot to include a field of information to hold each employee's sex. Although it is better to include all the necessary fields when creating the table structure, it is always possible to add or remove fields from a table at a later time. To change the table structure,

Choose: View>Table Structure
> ➢   ⇧ Shift + F2

or

Click: 📝 Modify Table

The table structure you defined in Lab 1 is displayed in the Table Structure window. After looking at the order of the fields, you decide to add the new field, SEX, between the ZIP_CODE and BIRTH_DATE fields.

To add the new field to the existing structure, a blank field line must be inserted between the eighth and ninth fields. To do this,

☞
The Insert Field command is
also on the SpeedMenu.

Move to: field 9, BIRTH_DATE

Choose: Structure>Insert Field

➤ Ctrl + N

The BIRTH_DATE field has moved down one line to become field number 10, and a blank field line is ready to be defined as field number 9.

Enter the new field information as follows:

Field name:	**SEX**
Type:	**Character**
Width:	**1**

Your screen should be similar to Figure 2-11.

Modify Table button

FIGURE 2-11

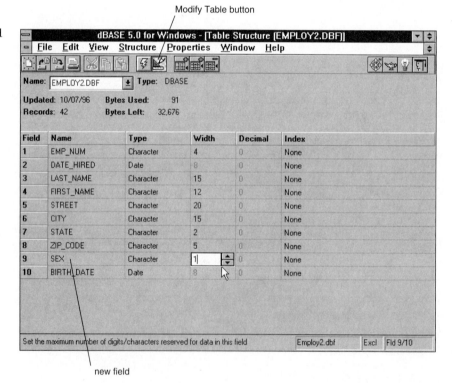

new field

To exit the Table Structure window and save the structure changes to the disk,

Choose: View>Table Records

➤ F2

or

Click: 🔗 View Table

A message box is displayed asking you to save the changes.

Choose: Yes

When you change the structure of a table, you often make changes that could result in a loss of data. Changes such as shortening field sizes or changing field types can cause existing data to become invalid. If this is the case, dBASE will display a dialog box warning you that data may be lost. Through careful analysis and design of your database, you can avoid having to change the structure of your table and risk the potential loss of data.

The disk-drive light goes on briefly as the changes to the file structure are saved on the disk. The new field has been added to the table.

Freezing a Field

You are now ready to enter the data for the SEX field for each record. The field value for each record will be either M for male or F for female. You can most likely tell the sex by looking at the employee's first name. For example, the first name for record 1 is William, therefore the SEX field value for record 1 should be M. If the name is not a good indicator of the person's sex, you could always verify the sex by checking the original employee data card.

Move to: SEX field for record 1

Both the FIRST_NAME and SEX fields are displayed on the screen. To enter the sex,

Press: Caps Lock
Type: M

The field value for the first record is entered as an uppercase M, and the selection bar moves to the BIRTH_DATE field. However, you do not want the selection bar to move to the next column. You want it to stay in the SEX field and move down to the next record so that you can enter the sex of the next employee. To keep the selection bar in the SEX field, you will **freeze** the field. To do this,

Choose: Properties>Table Records Window

The Table Records Properties dialog box is displayed. The tab folder that contains the Freeze option is Window. To display this folder,

> This option is also available on the SpeedMenu as Table Records Window Properties.

DATABASE

Choose: Window

The Window tab folder is displayed. To freeze the SEX field,

Choose: Freeze

> If you used the keyboard to select Freeze, press Alt + ↓ to display the drop-down list.

Your screen should be similar to Figure 2-12.

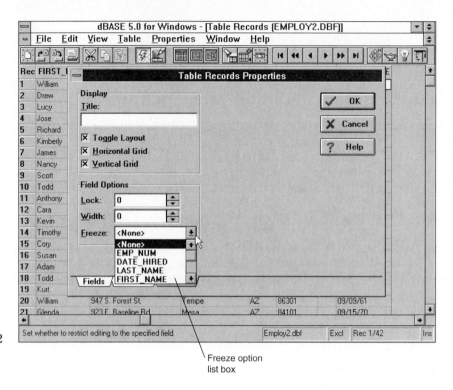

FIGURE 2-12

Freeze option
list box

From the drop-down list box,

Select: SEX
Choose: OK

The dialog box is closed and the selection bar is positioned in the SEX field. To enter
the employee's sex,

Type: M

The highlight moves down to the same field of the next record because the SEX field
is frozen. Freezing a field restricts editing to the frozen field.

Enter the Sex field values for the remaining records by looking at the first
name to determine whether the employee is male or female. When the Add Records
dialog box appears, choose No.

When you are done entering the SEX field values, to unfreeze the SEX field,

Choose: **P**roperties>**T**able Records Window>**F**reeze><None>>OK

The SEX field is no longer frozen.

Press: Caps Lock
Press: Ctrl + Page Up
Press: Ctrl + Home

Sorting Records

The accounting department has asked you to create an alphabetical list of all employees. As you recall from Lab 1, the records are displayed in the order they were entered into the table. This is called **natural order**. Natural order is sometimes referred to as data entry order or physical order. There are two ways to reorder records in a table, sorting and indexing. **Sorting** a table creates a new table with the records physically rearranged in the table and displayed in the order you specify. **Indexing** a table changes the display order of records, but does not create a new table or change the physical location of records in the table.

First you will use the Sort command to alphabetize the employee records.

Choose: <u>T</u>able><u>T</u>able Utilities><u>S</u>ort Records

Your screen should be similar to Figure 2-13.

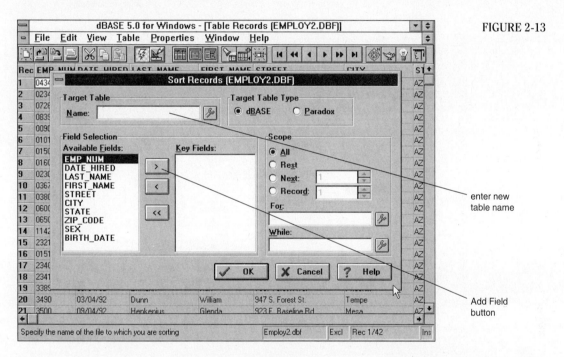

FIGURE 2-13

enter new table name

Add Field button

The Sort Records dialog box for the Employ2 table is displayed. First you need to specify a name for the table you will create. You can use the same file name, in which case the contents of the existing table will be replaced by the contents of the sorted table. Alternatively, you can create a new table file. To name the new table, in the Target Table Name text box,

Type: namesort (do not press ⏎Enter)

Next you select the field to sort on. The dialog box lists the field names in the Available Fields list box.

You can sort the records of a table according to the entries in one or more fields. You want the records arranged in alphabetical order by last name. But you would also like the records sorted so that any employees with the same last name will be sorted in order by first name.

As you select the field names, they will be displayed in the Key Field list box. As you learned in Lab 1, a key field controls the order in which records are displayed. To select the field names on which to sort the table, highlight the name. Then, to add it to the Key Fields list box, choose the ▣ Add Field button.

To specify a sort according to last name and then by first name, from the Available Fields list box,

Select: FIRST_NAME
Choose: ▸
Select: LAST_NAME
Choose: ▸

Your screen should be similar to Figure 2-14.

sorted table name   selected sort fields

FIGURE 2-14

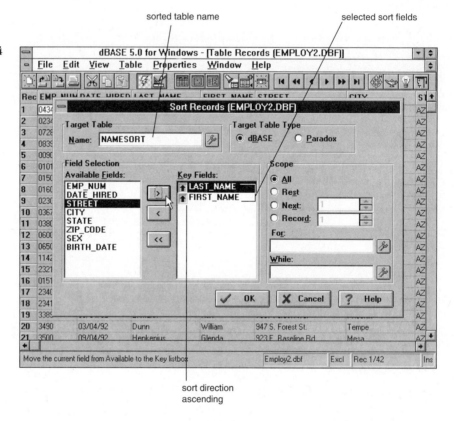

sort direction
ascending

You can double-click on the field name to add it to the Key Fields list. The fields are added to the top of the list as they are selected.

The two selected field names are displayed in the Key Fields list box. The order in which fields appear in the Key Fields list determines the order of the sort. The arrow ▲ to the left of the field name indicates the sort direction, in this case ascending (A to Z, 0 to 9). The direction can be changed to descending ▼ by choosing the arrow to display a drop-down list of the available sort options. By default, dBASE sorts in ascending order following these rules:

- Numeric fields are sequenced from lowest to highest number.
- Character fields are sequenced alphabetically according to the currently set sort order.

■ Memo fields, like character fields, are also sequenced alphabetically according to the currently set sort order; however, memo fields are sorted according to their initial display portions only.

■ Date fields are sequenced from earliest to latest date.

The default sort order, ascending, is acceptable. To complete the Sort,

Choose: OK

The drive light goes on and after a few seconds the sorted file is created and saved to the disk.
To view the records in the new table, you must open the table.

Choose: File>Open
➤ Ctrl + O
or
Click: 📁 Open
Choose: Namesort.dbf>OK

If necessary, maximize the Namesort window.
The employee names are listed in alphabetical order by last name. The record number associated with each record has changed, reflecting the record's new location in the table. The total count of records is the same.

Press: Page Down

Your screen should be similar to Figure 2-15.

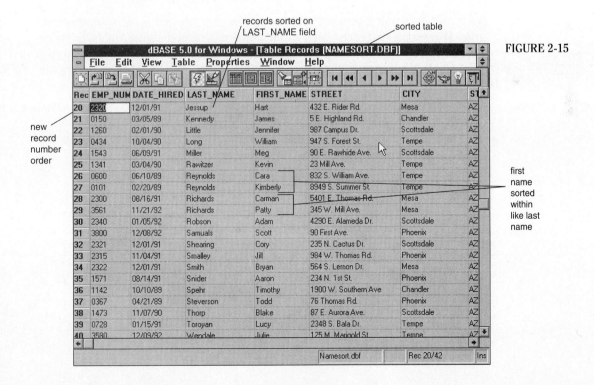

new record number order

records sorted on LAST_NAME field

sorted table

first name sorted within like last name

FIGURE 2-15

Those records with duplicate last names are further sorted by first names.

As you can see, sorting rearranges the data in the table in the order you need. However, as you will see, it has some limitations, especially when new records are added to the table.

You recently received data on a new employee and need to update the Namesort table by adding a new employee record.

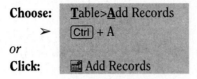

Choose: Table>Add Records

➤   Ctrl + A

or

Click: 📇 Add Records

A blank record row is displayed on the screen.
Enter the data shown below.

Field	Value
EMP_NUM	4210
HIRE_DATE	060795
LAST_NAME	Fisher
FIRST_NAME	Sarah
STREET	4720 N. Hobson Dr.
CITY	Mesa
STATE	AZ
ZIP_CODE	84101
SEX	F
BIRTH_DATE	121672

The record for Sarah Fisher is the last record in the table and is not in alphabetical order. This means that each time you add a new record to the sorted table, the table must be resorted to maintain the alphabetical order. In addition, the original file, Employ2, does not contain the record for Sarah Fisher. The new record would need to be added to this table too in order for the table to be current.

Close the Namesort table.

As you can see, the Sort command has some serious drawbacks:

■ Each time a table is sorted, a new file is created. With a large table, this duplication of data uses a lot of your disk space.

■ Sorting a large table takes a lot of time, sometimes several hours.

■ Each time a change, addition, or deletion is made to the original table, the sorted table becomes out of date. The original table would need to be resorted, or the sorted table would need to be updated.

For these reasons, using the Sort command is usually limited to tables that do not change frequently. Sort is not the best option for alphabetizing the employee table because records are added and deleted from the table frequently.

Indexing a Table

As mentioned earlier, another way to reorder a table is by creating an index. An index controls the order in which records are displayed, without changing their physical location in the table.

You want to create a simple index for the table that will display the records in order by last names. To do this,

Choose: Underline{V}iew>Table Underline{S}tructure
> ⟨⇧Shift⟩ + ⟨F2⟩

or

Click: 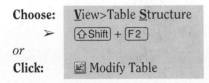 Modify Table

The Table Structure window is displayed. You want to index the table on the LAST_NAME field.

Move to the Index column of the LAST_NAME field.

To display the index order options,

Click: ⊞

or

Press: ⟨Alt⟩ + ⟨↓⟩

You would like the table in ascending order.

Choose: Ascend

Your screen should be similar to Figure 2-16.

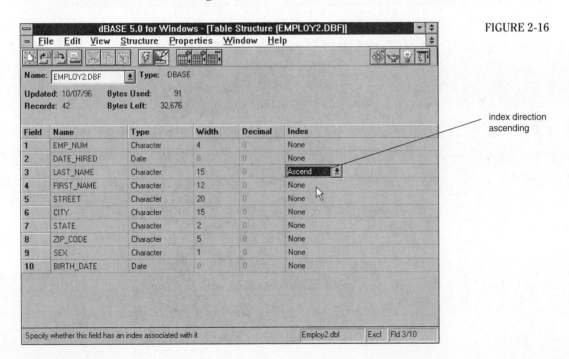

FIGURE 2-16

To return to the Table Records window,

Choose: <u>V</u>iew><u>T</u>able Records
➤   F2

or

Click: View Table

A message box is displayed, asking if you want to save current changes. To save the change,

Choose: <u>Y</u>es

Nothing appears different in the table until you apply the new index. To do this,

Choose: <u>T</u>able><u>T</u>able Utilities><u>M</u>anage Indexes

The original natural order index and the new LAST_NAME index are displayed in the dialog box.

Select: LAST_NAME
Choose: OK

Your screen should be similar to Figure 2-17.

FIGURE 2-17

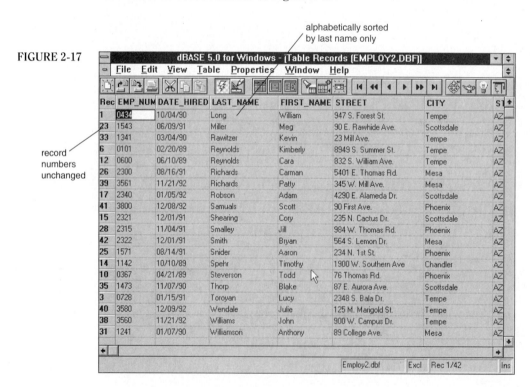

alphabetically sorted
by last name only

record numbers unchanged

The table has changed to display the records in alphabetical order by last name. Notice that the record numbers have not changed. Also notice that the records for Cara and Kimberly Reynolds are not in order by first name. You would like to further index the table on the FIRST_NAME field. To add this field to the LAST_NAME index,

Choose: Table>Table Utilities>Manage Indexes>Modify

Your screen should be similar to Figure 2-18.

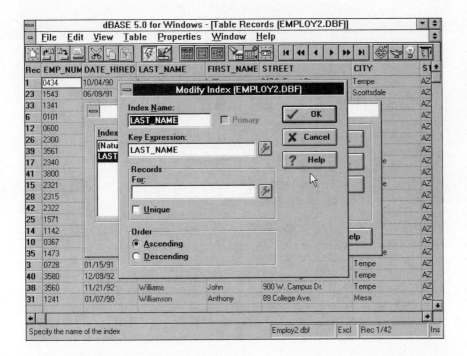

FIGURE 2-18

You need to change the index key expression to include the FIRST_NAME field.

Choose: Key Expression

The 🔧 to the right of the Key Expression text box will open the Edit an Expression dialog box.

Choose: 🔧

The Edit an Expression dialog box displays the expression in the text box and three list boxes. To add the FIRST_NAME field to the expression,

Press: →
Type: +

Click 🔧 or press Tab⇆ to move to 🔧 and press ↵Enter.

DATABASE

The Category list box displays the categories of elements that can be added to an expression. Because Field is the selected category, the field names in the table are displayed in the Paste list box. To paste the FIRST_NAME field into the expression,

Choose: P̲aste
Select: FIRST_NAME

To add the selected field to the expression, double-click the field name, drag the field name to the text box, or press (Spacebar). The field name will be entered into the expression at the location of the insertion point.
Using any of these methods, add the selected field to the end of the expression. Your screen should be similar to Figure 2-19.

FIGURE 2-19

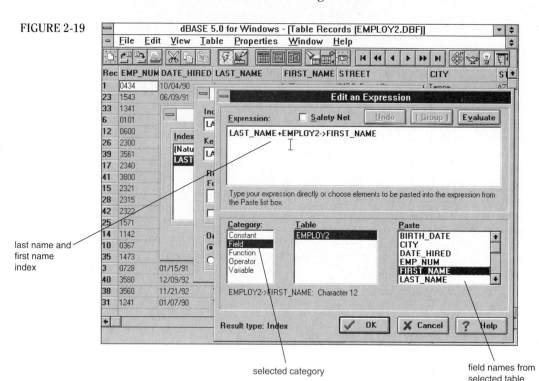

last name and
first name
index

selected category

field names from
selected table

Choose: OK

The modified index expression is displayed in the Expression text box. To close the dialog box,

Choose: OK

To close the Manage Indexes dialog box,

Choose: OK

After a few seconds, the table is organized in ascending order by last and first names. To see the next page of records,

Press: Page Down

The records for Reynolds and Richards are also in correct alphabetical order by first names. If you wanted to change the order back to the natural order, you would need to choose the Manage Indexes command again and select the Natural Order index.

Updating Indexed Tables

Now you will add the data for Sarah Fisher to the Employ2 table. (Remember, her record was added only to the sorted table, Namesort.)

Unlike a sorted database table, whenever you modify or add records to an indexed database file, dBASE automatically updates all indexes that are maintained.

Choose: Table>Add Records
➤ Ctrl + A
or
Click: 🖼 Add Records

A blank record row at the end of the file is displayed. Enter the data for Sarah Fisher exactly as it appears below:

Field	Value
EMP_NUM	4310
HIRE_DATE	060795
LAST_NAME	Fisher
FIRST_NAME	Sarah
STREET	4720 N. Hobson Dr.
CITY	Mesa
STATE	AZ
ZIP_CODE	84101
SEX	F
BIRTH_DATE	121672

To display the new record in index order,

Press: ↑

Your screen should be similar to Figure 2-20.

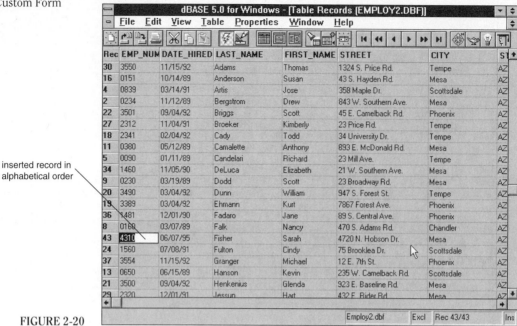

inserted record in
alphabetical order

FIGURE 2-20

The record is in the correct alphabetical order. Check the record for accuracy and edit it if necessary.

Note: If you are running short on time to complete this lab, this is an appropriate place to end this session. Close the Employ2 table and exit the program.

Creating a Customized Form

New records must be frequently added to the table. The input for the table comes from the Employee Data Form that each employee fills out when hired. The form looks like this:

Employee Data Form

Personal Data
First Name:_____ Last Name: _____
Street Address: _____
City: _____ State: _____ Zip:_____
Sex:_____ Birth Date: _____

Company Data
Employee #: _____
Hire Date: _____

As you can see, the order of information in the Employee Data Form is different than the order in which the data is entered in the table. To make the job of data entry easier, you decide to create a customized, onscreen data entry form, reflecting the order of the paper form, to be used to enter the data into the table.

The Form layout you viewed in Lab 1 is the default form style. This style can be changed to meet your needs by allowing you to create and save a customized entry form. Forms are designed primarily for onscreen use and are invaluable for simplifying data entry tasks.

Because the table was opened with exclusive use, you have to close it before creating the form.

Close the Employ2 table.

To create a form for entering data into the Employ2 table,

Choose: File>New>Form

The Form Expert dialog box is displayed. You can use the Form Expert to help you create a form or use a blank form to create a form from scratch. Form Expert prompts you about the form you want and then builds the form based on your answers. You would like to use the Form Expert to create the form. To do this,

Choose: Next

First, you need to specify the table whose data you want to use in your form. The File Name list box displays the available tables.

Choose: **Employ2.dbf**
Choose: Next

Your screen should be similar to Figure 2-21.

You can also click ⬜ New File and then choose Form.

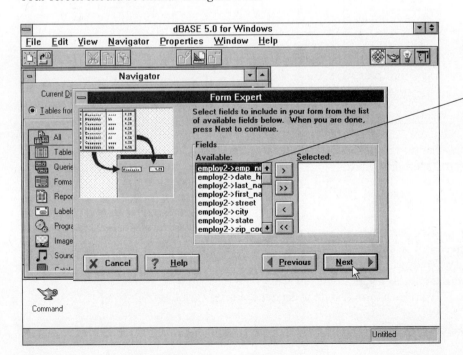

FIGURE 2-21

available fields

DATABASE

The next Form Expert dialog box is used to specify the fields you want included in the form. You want to add all the fields in the Employ2 table to the form. When adding fields to the form, the fields should be selected in the order you want them displayed on the form. The first field you would like to add to the form is the FIRST_NAME field. To do this, from the Available list box,

Select: FIRST_NAME

To place the field name in the Selected list box,

Choose: >

The FIRST_NAME field is removed from the Available list box and added to the Selected list box.
To add the next field to the Selected list, from the Available list,

Select: LAST_NAME
Choose: >

The LAST_NAME field is added to the Selected list below the FIRST_NAME field. If you add a field to the Selected list in the wrong order, remove it from the list using < . Then move the Selected list highlight to the field above the location where you want the field inserted, and add the field to the Selected list again.
In a similar manner, add the rest of the fields to the Selected list box in the following order:

Field
STREET
CITY
STATE
ZIP_CODE
SEX
BIRTH_DATE
EMP_NUM
DATE_HIRED

Now that all the fields are entered into the Selected list box, to move to the next Form Expert dialog box,

Choose: Next

This dialog box displays four sample design layouts for the form. Notice that the first three form layouts are the same as the table layout. The only new layout is One-To-Many. This layout is used when you are creating a form for two tables. You will learn more about this layout in the next lab.
To create a form using the default Columnar layout form,

Choose: Next

The table name precedes the field name in the list boxes.

Click > or use Tab ⇆ to move to the > button and press Spacebar.

The >> button will place all the fields in the table on a form in the same order they are displayed in the table.

The next Form Expert dialog box allows you to change the colors and type style and sizes of the items on the form. The default settings are displayed in the sample form and are acceptable. To create the form,

Choose: Create

dBASE now displays two new windows, Form Designer and Controls. The Form Designer window displays the form with the fields in the selected order and layout. The data for the current record is displayed in the form. In addition, the table name has been used as the form title. The Controls window displays the different types of objects that can be added to a form. You will learn more about the objects later in the lab.

To see more of the Form Design, maximize the Form Designer window. Your screen should be similar to Figure 2-22.

> A third window, Properties, may also be displayed.

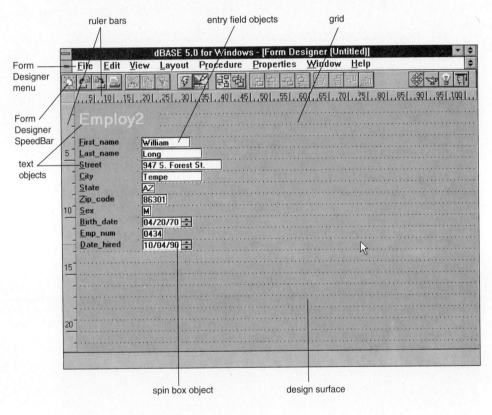

FIGURE 2-22

Selecting and Moving Objects

The Form Designer menu and SpeedBar display commands and buttons that are used to create or modify the form design. The window is bordered along the top and left sides by horizontal and vertical **ruler bars**. The rulers are used to help in placing items in the Form window. The **grid** or matrix of dots is used to help place items on the form.

The different parts of the form are called objects. **Objects** are design elements that consist of properties that can be modified. This form contains three types of objects: text, entry fields, and spin boxes. The form title and field names are **text** objects. The properties of this object are descriptive elements consisting of alphanumeric characters that can be edited by the user. The spaces where the field values are displayed are the **entry field** objects. These areas are designed to accept entry of data typed in by the user. The **spin box** objects are entry field objects that accept numeric values either by typing in the value or using the to increase or decrease the number. The form background, also called the **design surface,** is another object.

In the Form Designer window, an object can be selected and modified. When an object is selected, it is surrounded by black boxes called **selection handles**. How an object is selected varies if you are using a mouse or the keyboard.

To select an object, click on it.

Click on the form title.

To select an object, press [Tab↹]. [Tab↹] moves the selection handles forward from one object to another in sequence.

Press: [Tab↹]

The [⇧Shift] + [Tab↹] key combination will cycle backward through the objects.

Your screen should be similar to Figure 2-23.

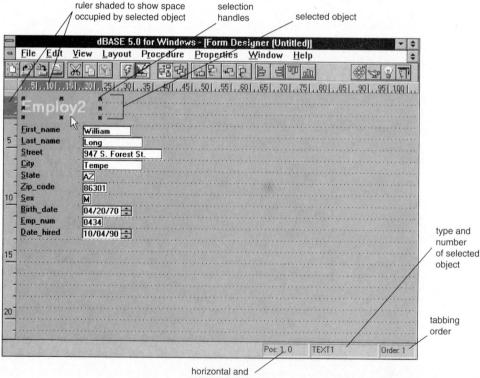

FIGURE 2-23

The form title is the selected object. The title is surrounded by eight handles, and the ruler is shaded to show the position of the selected object in the window. The status bar shows your horizontal and vertical position in the form as "Pos: 1,0." In addition, the status bar displays "TEXT1," which indicates that the selected object is a text object and that it was the first text object placed on the form. The last item in the status bar is "Order: 1." This indicator tells you the **tabbing order** of the object. Tabbing order is the order in which you move from one object to the next in the form when you press [Tab ⇄].

To select the next object on the form,

Click: FIRST_NAME field name
or
Press: [Tab ⇄]

The FIRST_NAME field name object is displayed at position 1 of line 3 in the form. This object is the second text object (TEXT2) on the form and is the second object in the tabbing order (Order: 2). To select the next object,

Click: FIRST_NAME entry field
or
Press: [Tab ⇄]

This object is the first entry field object (ENTRYFIELD1). It is the third object on the form in the tabbing order (Order: 3). The field names and entry fields are separate objects so that they can be moved independently on the form.

Once an object is selected, it can be modified. For example, you can modify an object by changing its size or location on the form. You would like to rearrange the objects in the form as in Figure 2-24.

> You can also delete a selected text object by pressing [Delete].

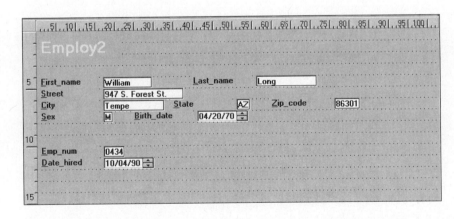

First_name   William   Last_name   Long
Street   947 S. Forest St.
City   Tempe   State   AZ   Zip_code   86301
Sex   M   Birth_date   04/20/70

Emp_num   0434
Date_hired   10/04/90

FIGURE 2-24

First you want to position the FIRST_NAME and LAST_NAME fields on the same line. To begin, you will move the LAST_NAME field name and entry field to the right to make space for the FIRST_NAME field.

To do this, select the LAST_NAME entry field object.

To move a selected object, you can drag the object with the mouse or use the navigation keys. When moving a selected object, use the ruler for location reference to help you align the rows and columns of fields. As the object is moved, the shaded area in the ruler shows your location in the window.

DATABASE

Drag or use the →⃞ key to move the LAST_NAME entry field object to the right on the same line (4) so it begins at position 55 on the horizontal ruler bar.

In the same manner, select the LAST_NAME field name object and move it to the right so it begins at position 40 on the horizontal ruler bar.

Your screen should be similar to Figure 2-25.

> To drag an object, point to the selected object (not a selection handle), hold down the left mouse button, and move the pointer. The pointer changes to a hand and an outline of the selected object moves as you move the mouse.

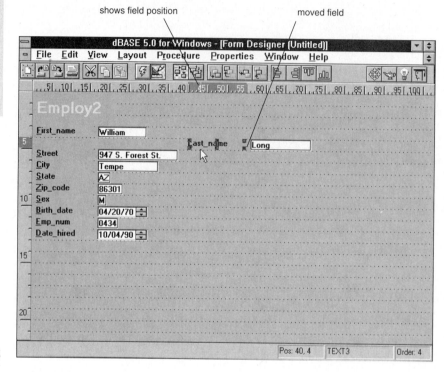

FIGURE 2-25

Next you would like to move the FIRST_NAME field name and entry field to the same line as the LAST_NAME field objects.

An advantage of using the mouse is that you can select several objects at the same time. This is called **multiselecting**. Then you can move all the selected objects as a group. To select multiple objects, press and hold down ⇧Shift⃞, then click each object. When you have selected the objects you want, release ⇧Shift⃞.

Click: FIRST_NAME field name object

Hold down ⇧Shift⃞.

Click: FIRST_NAME field entry object

Release ⇧Shift⃞.

Both objects are selected.

Drag the FIRST_NAME field objects down one row to row 4 and to the same position horizontally (beginning at position 1). Release the mouse button.

> If the mouse pointer is positioned on a selection handle, it appears as a two-headed arrow. This indicates you can drag the mouse to change the *size* of the selected object.

Select and move the FIRST_NAME field name object and entry field object down one line to row 4 to the same horizontal positions as they were on line 3.

Your screen should be similar to Figure 2-26.

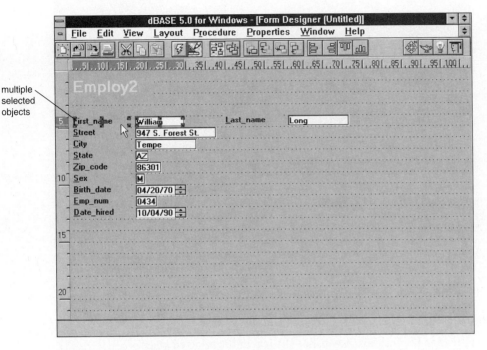

multiple
selected
objects

FIGURE 2-26

In the same manner, move the other fields to the positions shown in Figure 2-24. Do not be concerned if rows and columns do not line up exactly.

Enhancing the Form

Now that all the fields are positioned how you want them on the form, you want to change the form title to be more descriptive of the form's content.

Select the form title.

All objects consist of attributes called **properties**. To change the properties associated with an object, the Properties window is used.

Choose: View

If the Object Properties option is checked, the window is already open. Cancel the menu and select Properties from the Window menu to display the window. If the window is maximized, restore it to its previous size.

If Object Properties is not checked, to open the window,

Choose: Object Properties

The Object Properties command is also on the SpeedMenu.

DATABASE

Your screen should be similar to Figure 2-27.

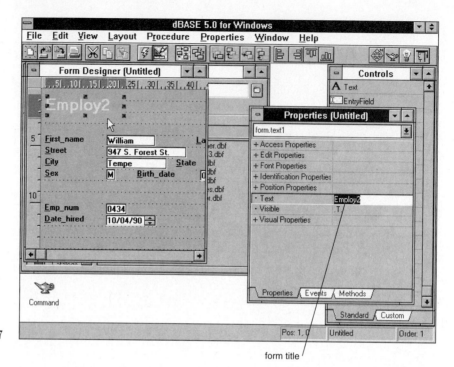

FIGURE 2-27

form title

The Properties tab dialog box is displayed. If the Properties folder is not open, open it.

Notice that the default text in this object, the table name Employ2, is highlighted in the text box. To change the text of the selected object,

Type: The Sports Company Employee Record

The new text appears in the form in the Form Designer window as you type it in the text box.

To view the whole form again, maximize the Form Designer window.

The form title object is not large enough to display the new title. You need to adjust the size of the title object.

Point to a handle on the right side of the title object.

The mouse pointer changes to a ⇔.

Drag the title object border until the entire title is displayed.

To size an object, press and hold ⇧Shift while pressing a directional key.

Press: ⇧Shift + → until the title is fully displayed

Your screen should be similar to Figure 2-28.

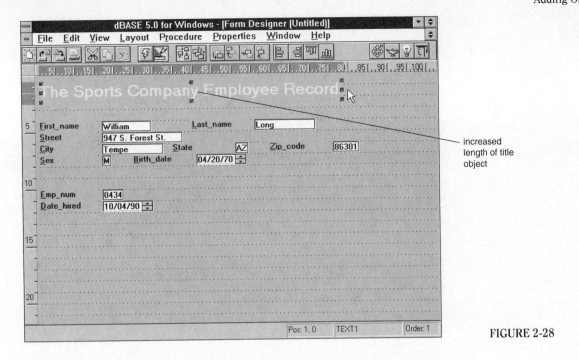

increased
length of title
object

FIGURE 2-28

To center the title over the form, move the title to the right so it begins at position 5 on the horizontal ruler.

Adding Objects to a Form

You can also add other objects to the form. You will add two text objects to the form. The first will display the text PERSONAL DATA above the FIRST_NAME field and the second will display the text COMPANY DATA above the employee number field. The Controls window is used to add objects to a form. This window is already open. To display the Controls window,

Choose: Window>Controls

DATABASE

Your screen should be similar to Figure 2-29.

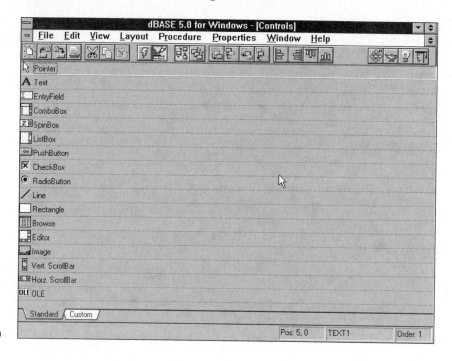

FIGURE 2-29

The Controls window lists the different types of objects that can be added to a form. The **A** Text Text tool is used to add a text object to the form.

Double-click **A** Text or move to **A** Text and press ←Enter to insert the text field on the form.

Choose: **A** Text

The Controls window status bar indicates you have added object Text12 to the form in the 22 tab order position. To see the object that was added to the form,

Choose: Window>Form Designer

The object Text12 is the selected object and appears in the form wherever the insertion point was last positioned in the form. Now you need to move the text object to the location in the form where you want the text displayed.

Move the Text12 selected object to position 1 of line 3. (Refer to the status bar for position location.)

Next you want to change the default text for this object to PERSONAL DATA. To enter the new text for the text object,

Choose: Window>Properties

The Properties window displays the default text for the selected object. To replace the default text label,

Type: **PERSONAL DATA**

To return to the Form Designer window to see the new text in the form,

Choose: Window>Form Designer

The new text is too large to be fully displayed.
Adjust the size of the text box until the entire entry is displayed.
Your screen should be similar to Figure 2-30.

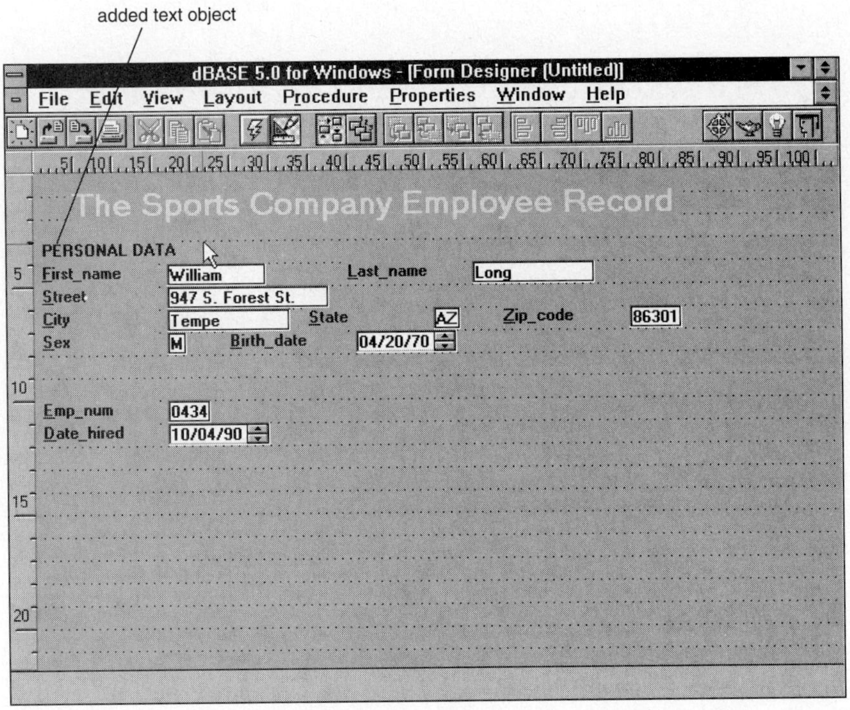

added text object

FIGURE 2-30

Add the next text object (Text13) to the form. Move the object to position 1 on line 9 and change the text in the text object to COMPANY DATA.

Entering Data in the Custom Form

Now you would like to use the form to enter a new record. To change to Form view,

Choose: View>Form
➢ F2
or
Click: 🕒 Run Form

The Save Form dialog box is displayed. You want to save the form with the name PERDATA. In the File Name text box,

Type: PERDATA
Choose: OK

The form is saved as PERDATA with the file extension .WFM.

Your screen should be similar to Figure 2-31.

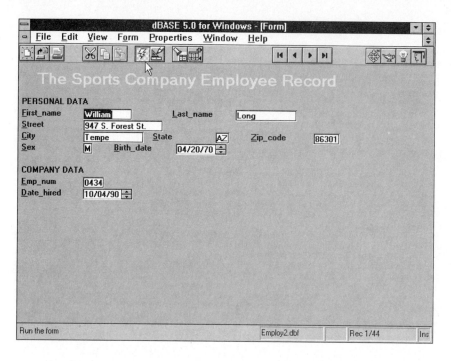

FIGURE 2-31

The custom form is displayed in Form layout and can now be used to modify table records. The data for the first record in the table is displayed in the customized entry form. To add a new record,

Choose: Form>Add Records
➢   Ctrl + A

Enter a record using your special employee number, 9999, and your first and last names. The data in all other fields can be fictitious, except enter the current date as your date hired.

Switch to the Navigator window. Open the Employ2 table.

The table is opened and displays the records in natural order. Your record should have been entered in the table as the last record. Display your record and edit any errors if necessary.

Using the form will make entering the new employee data much faster.

Switch back to the Form window and print the form containing your name (File>Print). Close the Form and Table windows.

To leave dBASE,

> Use the Window menu or click ▥ to switch to the Navigator.

Choose: File>Exit

Reminder: Do not remove your data disk from the drive until you close the dBASE applications window.

Exit Windows.

Key Terms

SpeedMenu (DB49)
pack (DB52)
tab dialog box (DB53)
freeze (DB59)
natural order (DB61)
sort (DB61)
index (DB61)
ruler bar (DB73)
grid (DB73)

object (DB73)
text (DB73)
entry field (DB74)
spin box (DB74)
design surface (DB74)
selection handles (DB74)
tabbing order (DB75)
multiselect (DB76)
property (DB77)

Command Summary

Command	Shortcut	SpeedBar	Action
Table>**D**elete Selected Record	Ctrl + U		Marks selected record for deletion
Table>**T**able Utilities>**P**ack Records			Erases marked files
Table>**F**ind Records	Ctrl + F		Locates records in file
Edit>**U**ndo	Ctrl + Z		Cancels last action
Structure>**I**nsert Field	Ctrl + N		Inserts new field in Design layout
Properties>**T**able Records Window>**F**reeze			Freezes and unfreezes field columns
Table>**T**able Utilities>**S**ort Records			Arranges records into a new file
Table>**T**able Utilities>**M**anage Indexes			Applies and modifies indexes
File>**N**ew>**F**orm			Creates new form
View>**O**bject Properties			Changes properties associated with an object
View>**F**orm	F2		Displays table in Form layout
F**o**rm>**A**dd Records	Ctrl + A		Adds record to form

DATABASE

Matching

1. freeze	_____	**a.** changes display order of a table
2. selection handles	_____	**b.** adds a record to a table
3. object	_____	**c.** black boxes that surround a selected object
4. 🖼	_____	**d.** permanently reorders records of a table
5. Undo	_____	**e.** order in which records were originally entered
6. index	_____	**f.** design document used primarily for onscreen display
7. sort	_____	**g.** restores any changes made to current record
8. Ctrl + F	_____	**h.** restricts editing to a specified field
9. natural order	_____	**i.** locates records in file
10. form	_____	**j.** a design element that consists of properties that can be modified

Practice Exercises

1.   Audra forgot to include a field to enter her friends' and relatives' birthdays, and she also found some corrections to the information she already entered. Open the file Friends, which you created in Practice Exercise 1 of Lab 1.

  a.   Add the new field BIRTHDATE as the last field in the table structure.

  b.   Lock the BIRTHDATE field and enter the following birthdays for the records:

Record	Birthdate
1	09/15/70
2	04/06/73
3	07/17/68
4	08/06/70
5	(your birthdate)

  c.   Use the Find Records command to locate the following records, then edit the records.

Locate	Field	Correction
Bell	BIRTHDATE	09/25/73
Pliney	LAST_NAME	Delder
Sanchez	PHONE_NUM	602-555-9090

  d.   Index the table by last name.

Audra decides that it would be more efficient to create a form to give to her friends and family to fill out.

    e.   Create a customized form design of your choice. Save the form as Dataform.

    f.   Enter the following records using the customized form:

Record 6	Record 7
Leighty	Kramer
Melyssa	Jay
1455 N. French Way	124 N. Campus Dr.
Glendale	Tempe
AZ	AZ
85645	85222
602-555-1342	602-555-1212
10/12/68	10/05/75

    g.   Print the indexed table and form of your record.

2. Sam manages the Appliance Company and has been using dBASE to create a table of employee records. In this problem you will use features you learned in the lab to modify the table.

    a.   Open the table Appco.

    b.   Use the Find Record command to locate the following records, then edit the records.

Locate	Field	Correction
Melissa Reynolds	Last name	Kelly
Employee Number 324	Address	90 E. Southern Ave.
Dean Hayes	City	Westwood
Employee Number 2349	State	PA
Byron Baker	Last name	Weston

    c.   Convert the state field to all uppercase letters. *Hint:* Since there is more than one state in the table, use the Single Replace option.

    d.   Enter your name in the last record of the table.

    e.   Create a sorted table by last and first name.

    f.   Open and print the sorted table.

3. Kevin Henderson has created a dBASE table to record the customers for his mail order office supply business. He would like to organize the table and create a data entry form.

    a.   Open the table Office.

    b.   Index the table on the customer name field.

    c.   Order the table using the customer index.

    d.   Create a customized form design of your choice. Save the form as Ofform.

e. Using the form, enter the following records into the table.

CUST_NUM	CUST_NAME	STREET	CITY	STATE	ZIP_CODE
310	A-D-C Pumps	381 E. Kansas St.	Kansas City	KS	45293
912	Apple Appliances	90 South St.	Keene	NH	03892
529	Venture Works	31 Temple Dr.	Portland	OR	74321

f. Enter yourself as the last customer in the table. Enter your name in the CUST_NAME field. The rest of the information can be fictitious.

g. Print the table. Print the form with your record displayed.

4. James is the owner of The Gift Center. He has created a table to hold the store's inventory. You have been hired as inventory control manager and will use the database to create weekly summaries of the data.

a. Open the table Giftctr. Edit the item names that have irregular-case words and misspellings.

b. Mark the following records for deletion:
record 17
record 15
record 3

c. Display the Delete column. Check to make sure that only the above records are marked for deletion. Pack the file. Turn off the display of the Delete column.

d. Search the table for the Yamaha Drum Machine and change the price to $129.00.

e. Enter your name as a new record. Use the number 999999 as the item number. Complete the other fields with data of your choice.

f. Index the table on the description. Order the table using the index.

g. Create a customized form using a design layout of your choice. Save the form as Giftform.

h. Print the table. Print the form with your record displayed.

You will continue this problem as Practice Exercise 3 in Lab 3.

5. Pam is the manager of Travel Abroad, a small travel agency specializing in group tours. One of Pam's responsibilities is to enter trips sold by the sales staff into the computer.

a. Create a table to hold the trips sold. Include the following fields:

Field Name	Type	Size
EMP_NUM	Character	3
CUST_ID	Character	5
TICKET_NUM	Character	6
TRIP_DEST	Character	15
TRAV_DATE	Date	
RETN_DATE	Date	

    b.   Save the table as Trips.

    c.   Enter four records into the table. So that your name will appear in the final printout, include your name as one of the destinations. Use the following numbers as the Emp #'s: 234, 245, 342, and 311.

    d.   Index the table by TRIP_DEST in ascending order.

    e.   Using a design layout of your choice, create a customized form for use in entering the data for trips sold. Enhance the form by adding a descriptive title and text. Save the form using a name of your choosing.

    f.   Using the form, enter five more records into the table. Use the following numbers as the Emp #'s: 234, 245, 342, and 311.

    g.   Print the form containing your name.

    h.   Order the table by the index. Print the entire table.

You will use this table in Practice Exercise 1 of Lab 3.

6.   Create an inventory table for The Lights That Shine lighting store. Include fields such as item number, description, order quantity, and price. Add five records to the table. Create a form using a design layout of your choice. Add five more records using the form. Index the table on Quantity. Print the indexed table. Add two new records to the table. Enter your name and the current date in one of the fields. Sort the table by the product description. Print the sorted table. Print the form displaying the record with your name.

CASE STUDY

Now that you have the database of employee records structured the way you want, you will use the information to answer questions and create a multitable form. You have also created several other tables that contain company data such as pay rates and job titles. You want to use the information in the tables to provide the answers to several inquiries about The Sports Company employees. You also want to create another customized form that will allow you to update records in multiple tables from one form.

Querying a Table

Load Windows. Put your data disk in drive A (or the appropriate drive for your system). Load dBASE for Windows.

You have continued to enter the employee records for the employee table. The updated table is Employ3 and now contains 70 records.

If necessary, change the default directory to the drive containing your data disk. Open the Employ3 table and maximize the table window.

Enter a record using your special employee number, 9999, and your first and last names. Enter the current date as your date hired. The data in all other fields can be fictitious.

Your first request for information from the Regional Manager is to provide a list of all employees in order by the date they were hired. Although the Employ3 table contains this information, you want the list to display only the employees' names and dates hired. To create this list, you can ask the table to provide the needed information.

Competencies

After completing this lab, you will know how to:

1. Query tables.
2. Move columns.
3. Query with wildcard operators.
4. Query with comparison operators.
5. Use logical ANDs and ORs.
6. Query for an exact match.
7. Create a calculated field.
8. Create a multitable form.

DATABASE

A question you ask about your database table is called a **query**. A query speci-
fies how dBASE should look at and organize the data. dBASE uses a query method
called **query by example** or **QBE**. You create a query by specifying the information
you want using the Query Designer window. Then you run the query to display the
results. The output is displayed in a temporary table called a **view**. The view is
displayed in the Query Results window and consists of the selected data from the table.

To specify the information to be displayed in the view, you must open the
Query Designer.

Choose: File>New>Query>EMPLOY3.DBF>OK
or
Click: 🖼 New Query

Your screen should be similar to Figure 3-1.

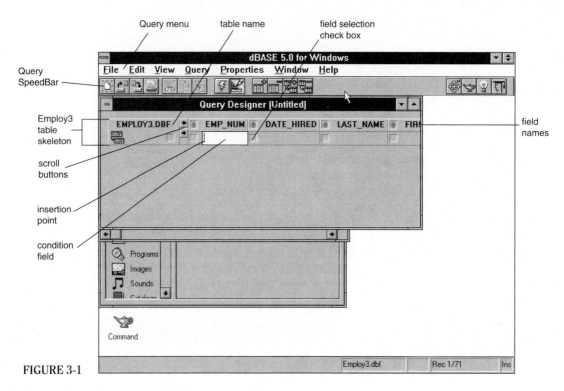

FIGURE 3-1

The Query Designer window is open with fields from the Employ3 table displayed in a row. The Query Designer has its own menu and set of SpeedBar buttons. The SpeedBar buttons are identified below.

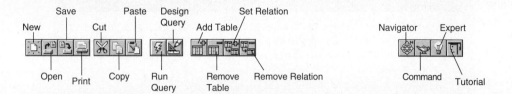

To see more of the Query Designer, maximize the window.

The Query Designer displays the fields from the Employ3 table in the same order as in the table. This is called a **skeleton** of the table structure. dBASE displays the table name at the left and the names of each field across a row. The space below each field name is where you will enter the instructions or specifications that dBASE will use to create the query view. The space includes a **field selection check box** and a text area called the **condition field**. You navigate through the fields and enter data into the fields the same way you would in a table. Currently, the EMP_NUM field is selected, and the insertion point is positioned below the EMP_NUM field name in the condition field.

If you want a field to appear in the view, you place a check mark in the field's selection check box. To enter a check mark, move to that field and press [F5] Check or click the field's selection check box. You want the view to display the DATE_HIRED, FIRST_NAME, and LAST_NAME fields. To specify the DATE_HIRED field,

Click: DATE_HIRED selection check box
or
Press: [Tab ⇆]
Press: [F5]

A check mark is displayed in the DATE_HIRED selection check box.

To tell dBASE to include the last and first name fields, place a check mark in each field's selection check box.

> Click the scroll button in the skeleton or use the [Tab ⇆] and [⇧ Shift] + [Tab ⇆] keys to scroll to the fields that are not visible in the window.

> If you accidentally place a check mark in the wrong field, click the field's check box again or press [F5] in the field to remove the check.

DATABASE

Your screen should be similar to Figure 3-2.

FIGURE 3-2

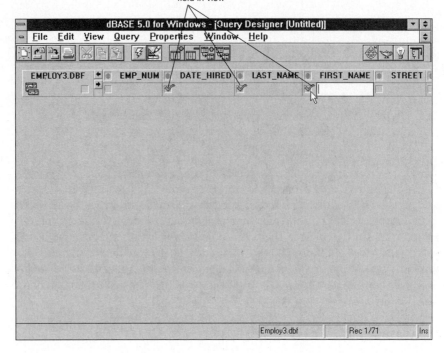

To run the query and display the results,

Choose: <u>V</u>iew>Query <u>R</u>esults
   ➢   F2
or
Click: 🔏 Run Query

After a few moments, the view is displayed in the Query Results window.

Your screen should be similar to Figure 3-3.

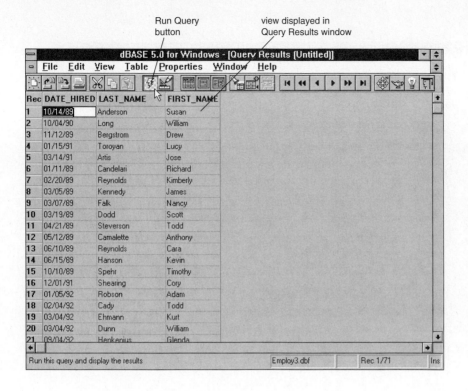

FIGURE 3-3

The view displays only the three fields whose field selection check boxes were checked for each record. The order of the fields in the view reflects the order they are checked in the Query Designer. The leftmost field that is checked in the skeleton is the leftmost field in the view.

Moving Columns

Note: If you do not have a mouse attached to your computer, skip to the next section, "Querying with Wildcards."

The Regional Manager wants the list of names organized with the first name before the last name. You can reformat the display of any table or query view by using the Move feature. When you move a column, you are not changing the format of the actual table or query. If you wanted to change the structure of the table, you would use the Design command on the Table menu.

To change the order of the columns, point to the column head of the column you want to move. When the mouse pointer changes to a hand ☜, you can drag the column to a new location in the query view. To move the LAST_NAME column to the right of the FIRST_NAME column,

Point to: LAST_NAME field column head

Drag the column outline to the right of the FIRST_NAME column.

DATABASE

Your screen should be similar to Figure 3-4.

FIGURE 3-4

moved column   hand mouse pointer

Rec	DATE_HIRED	FIRST_NAME	LAST_NAME
1	10/14/89	Susan	Anderson
2	10/04/90	William	Long
3	11/12/89	Drew	Bergstrom
4	01/15/91	Lucy	Toroyan
5	03/14/91	Jose	Artis
6	01/11/89	Richard	Candelari
7	02/20/89	Kimberly	Reynolds
8	03/05/89	James	Kennedy
9	03/07/89	Nancy	Falk
10	03/19/89	Scott	Dodd
11	04/21/89	Todd	Steverson
12	05/12/89	Anthony	Camalette
13	06/10/89	Cara	Reynolds
14	06/15/89	Kevin	Hanson
15	10/10/89	Timothy	Spehr
16	12/01/91	Cory	Shearing
17	01/05/92	Adam	Robson
18	02/04/92	Todd	Cady
19	03/04/92	Kurt	Ehmann
20	03/04/92	William	Dunn
21	09/04/92	Glenda	Henkenius

dBASE 5.0 for Windows - [Query Results (Untitled)]
File Edit View Table Properties Window Help

Employ3.dbf   Rec 1/71   Ins

The view is now displayed the way you would like it printed. If you wanted, you could print a copy of the view using the Print command on the File menu or 🖶 Print.

You can also move columns in the skeleton. This changes the display order of the view each time you run the query.

Querying with Wildcards

The Regional Manager received a memo on how the warehouse could save time and money by changing one of the reporting procedures it uses. However, the signature on the memo is illegible. The manager can read only the first letter of the last name in the signature. To figure out which employee sent the memo, you have been asked to create a list of all employees whose last names start with a C.

You could index the table on the LAST_NAME field and then write down all the employees' names. However, this could be very time consuming if you had hundreds of employees in the table. A faster way is to query the Employ3 table to find all the employees whose last names begin with the letter C.

First you must switch back to the Query Designer window. To do this,

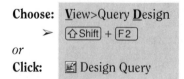

Choose: **V**iew>Query **D**esign
➤ ⟨⇧Shift⟩ + ⟨F2⟩
or
Click: 📝 Design Query

Since you no longer want the DATE_HIRED field displayed in the query results, you will remove the check from this field's selection checkbox. To do this,

Click:	DATE_HIRED selection check box
or	
Move to:	DATE_HIRED
Press:	F5

The first and last name fields are still marked.

Next you want to modify the existing query to locate those employees having a last name beginning with C. dBASE allows you to create a query that will select only the records that meet certain conditions. To do this, you use query **operators**. Operators consist of **reserved words** (words that have special meaning to the program) and symbols that allow you to specify conditions to be met. In this case, you will use the Like operator to search for a character pattern. In addition, you will use a wildcard operator. The **wildcard operators** are the symbols * and ?, and are the same as those you can use to locate files in DOS. The ? operator looks for any single character, while the * operator looks for any series of characters. You will use the operator * to find any characters that follow the letter C.

You will enter the conditions that you want records in the LAST_NAME field to meet by typing the conditions in the LAST_NAME condition field (the text area to the right of the check box). The following requirements apply when you enter query conditions in different field types:

Field Type	Requirement	Example
Character	Surround the text by double quotation marks (" "), single quotation marks (' '), or brackets ([ ]).	"S"
Numeric	Enter numbers exactly as they are entered in the table, including decimal points and negative signs.	5.00
Date	Enclose the date in curly braces ({ }).	{1/1/96}
Logical	Enter a period on both sides of the letter used to represent a logical value.	.T.
Memo	Enter a dollar sign before the text.	$"Smith"

DATABASE

If you enter a condition incorrectly, dBASE will beep and display the error in a yellow highlight. Correct the error using the editing features you learned in Lab 2 before continuing.

To locate all the employees whose last name begins with C,

Move to: LAST_NAME text area
Type: **like "C*"**

To run the query,

Choose: Vi̲ew>Query R̲esults
   ➤   [F2]
or
Click: ⚡ Run Query

Your screen should be similar to Figure 3-5.

FIGURE 3-5

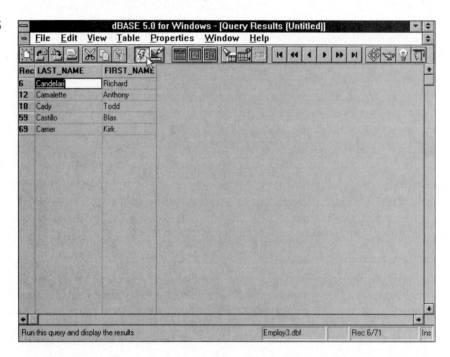

The Query Results window now displays the last and first names of all employees (five) whose last name begins with the letter C. Now the manager can determine which employee sent the memo. Notice that the fields are again displayed in the same order as they are in the skeleton. Because the view is a temporary table, any columns you may have moved in the last view are not moved in this view.

Querying Using Comparison Operators

The Regional Manager would like to start recognizing the employees with multiple years of service. To help the manager locate these employees, you will create a list of all employees who were hired before January of 1991.

> Switch to the Query Designer and check the DATE_HIRED field.

In the DATE_HIRED field you need to enter the condition to display only those records for employees whose date of hire is prior to January 1991. To create this list, you will revise the query statement by using a **comparison** or **relational operator** in the DATE_HIRED condition field. A comparison operator is used to select records within a range of values. The operators are identified in the table below:

Operator	Meaning
=	equal to (optional)
>	greater than
<	less than
>=	greater than or equal to
<=	less than or equal to

The = operator is always implied if no other operator is used. To make this comparison, you will use the less than (<) comparison operator. This operator will locate all records with a value less than the value you specify following the operator. In the DATE_HIRED condition field,

Type: `<{1/1/91}`

Finally, you need to remove the search condition from the LAST_NAME query skeleton field.

> Select the LAST_NAME condition.

Press: `Delete`

To run the query,

Choose: **V**iew>Query **R**esults
> `F2`
or
Click: Run Query

After a few moments, the view is displayed.

> To select the condition, double-click on the condition, drag, or use the `⇧Shift` + directional keys to highlight the text.

DATABASE

Your screen should be similar to Figure 3-6.

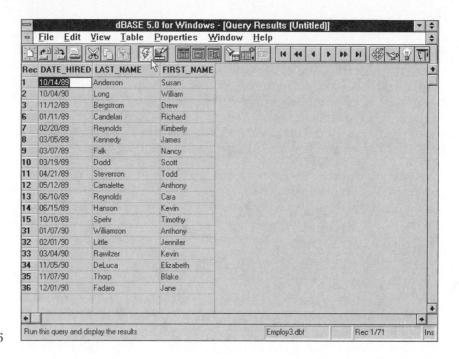

FIGURE 3-6

The view displays the names and hire dates for the 19 employees who were hired before January of 1991.

You created a printout of this list and gave it to the Regional Manager. The manager was busy, but indicated he would look at the printout in a few minutes and get back to you.

Using Logical ANDs and ORs

Many of the requests you get for information ask you to locate records using more than one condition. While waiting for your manager's comments, you decide to try creating a multiple-condition query. There are two kinds of multiple-condition queries. A query in which all conditions are met is called a **logical AND**, and a query in which either of two (or any of several) conditions are met is called a **logical OR**.

Switch to the Query Designer.

To see how these two types of operations work, you will first query the table to find all employees who have a hire date of 1/1/94 or later *and* live in the city of Mesa. When you enter conditions in separate condition fields on the same line of the query skeleton, a logical AND operation is established.

To create this query,

> The city condition of Mesa must be enclosed in quotes and must be entered exactly as it appears in the table.

- Change the Date Hired condition to >={1/1/94}.
- Enter "Mesa" as the condition in the CITY condition field.
- Place a check mark in the CITY field selection check box so it is displayed in the query view.

Your screen should be similar to Figure 3-7.

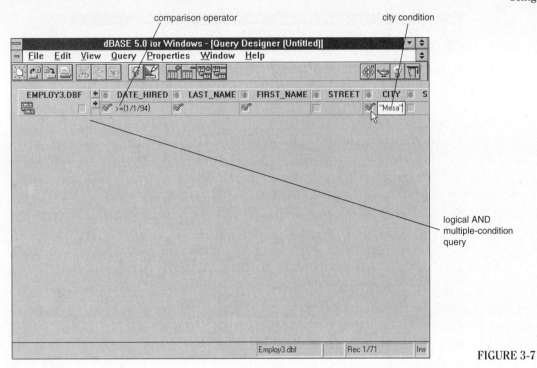

FIGURE 3-7

Run the query ([F2] or [🔏]).

The view shows that three employees were hired on or after January of 1994 and live in the city of Mesa.

You can also create a logical AND in a single field. The two conditions are separated by a comma, which acts as an AND operator. This requires that both of the conditions in the field be met. For example, the conditions >{1/1/55}, <{1/1/60} entered in the BIRTH_DATE field would locate all records that have a date greater than January 1, 1955, and less than January 1, 1960.

Next you want to see how many employees have this same hire date *or* live in the city of Mesa. When you enter conditions in separate fields on separate lines, a logical OR operation is established.

Switch to the Query Designer.

To create a second line in a query skeleton,

Press: [↓]

To create the OR operation, remove the city condition from the first line of the CITY condition field and enter it on the second line of the CITY condition field.

The Cut and Paste commands or 🖾 and 🖺 buttons can be used to move the condition from the first line to the second.

DATABASE

Your screen should be similar to Figure 3-8.

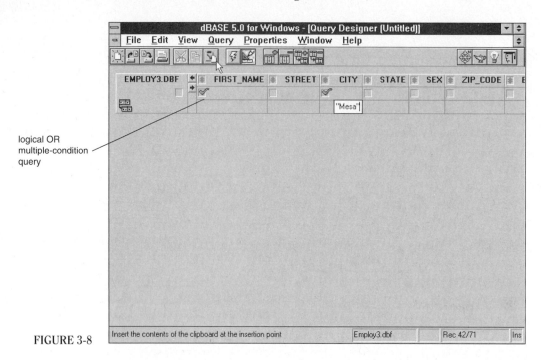

logical OR
multiple-condition
query

FIGURE 3-8

Run the query. The view shows all employees who live in the city of Mesa or were hired on or after January of 1994.

You can also create a logical OR in a single field. This requires that either condition in the field be met.

Close the Query Results window. When prompted to save the query, choose No.

Querying Two Tables

The Regional Manager has looked at the list of employees hired before January 1991, which you gave him earlier, and suggests that the query would be more helpful if it included each employee's department. Unfortunately, the Employ3 table does not contain this information. However, this information is available in another table named Position.

You would like to see the information in the Position table. To switch to the Navigator window,

Choose: **W**indow>**1** Navigator
or
Click: ⊞ Navigator

To open the Position table,

Choose: POSITION.DBF

Double-click on the table name or move the highlight to the table name and press ⏎Enter.

The Position table displays four fields of data: EMP_NUM, STORE_NUM, DEPART-MENT, and JOB_TITLE. To create a query that will display the information the

Regional Manager wants, you will join or **link** the two tables together in the Query Designer window and create a query using the information from both tables.

A query that uses more than one table is called a **multitable query**. The ability to link tables is the basis for relational databases. Rather than creating one large and cumbersome table containing all the fields of data, you can create several smaller and more manageable tables containing related data. Then as the need arises, you can link the tables to create output that combines the information from several tables.

Tables to be linked must have at least one field in common. The fields must be of the same type but can have different field names. Both tables must have key fields. Key fields are created by adding an index to the field you will use to create the link. In this case the common field is EMP_NUM.

dBASE searches the linked fields for exact matches of data in order to combine the information from several tables into one table in the view. The table you are linking from is called the **parent table**, and the table you are linking to is called the **child table**.

The diagram below shows that when the EMP_NUM fields of two tables are linked in a query, a view can be created using data from both tables.

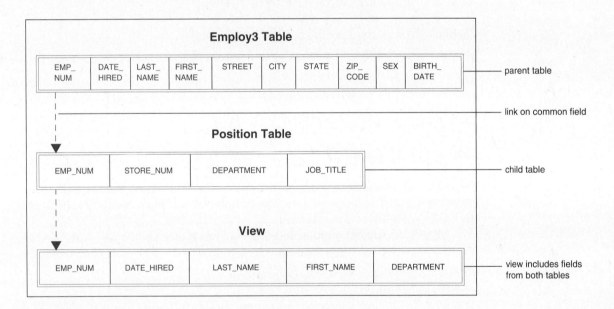

The Employ3 table and the Position table have the EMP_NUM field as the common field. However, both tables do not have an index on this field.

To create an index on the EMP_NUM field of the Position table,

Choose: <u>V</u>iew><u>T</u>able Structure

    ➤   ⇧ Shift + F2

or

Click: 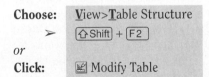 Modify Table

To open the table for exclusive use and set the index for the table,

Choose:	**O**pen Exclusive
Move to:	Index column of EMP_NUM field
Choose:	Ascend

To return to the Table Records window,

Choose:	**V**iew>**T**able Records
➤	F2
or	
Click:	⚡ Run Table

To save the modification to the table,

Choose:	**Y**es

Next you need to add an index to the Employ3 table.

Choose:	**W**indow>**3** Table Records [EMPLOY3.DBF]
Choose:	**V**iew>**T**able Structure
or	
Click:	✎ Modify Table

To open the table for exclusive use,

Choose:	**O**pen Exclusive

This table also contains an index on the LAST_NAME field, just like the index you created in Lab 2. The Index column displays None for the LAST_NAME field because the LAST_NAME index is not selected.

dBASE can support multiple indexes. To create a second index,

Move to:	Index column of EMP_NUM field
Choose:	Ascend

Return to the Table view and save the changes.

Because the tables were opened with exclusive use, you have to close them before creating the query.

Close the Employ3 and Position tables.

The Navigator window is displayed. To query information from more than one table, you must first determine the format for the output. dBASE will display first, in the leftmost columns, the information from the first table opened in the Query Designer window before information in subsequently opened tables. If you want the view to display records sorted by a certain field, first open the table in the Query Designer window containing that field and choose the field as the first field.

You are now ready to create a query using two tables. You want the view to display the information in the Employ3 table in the leftmost columns; therefore, you will select this table first. To create a new query,

Choose:	File>New
or	
Click	▣ New File
Choose:	Query>EMPLOY3.DBF>OK

The query skeleton for the Employ3 table is displayed.
Maximize the Query Designer window.
To open a second table in the Query Designer window,

> You can also select "Untitled" from the Queries group to create a new query.

Choose:	Query>Add Table
➤	Ctrl + A
or	
Click:	▦ Add Table
Choose:	POSITION.DBF>OK

Your screen should be similar to Figure 3-9.

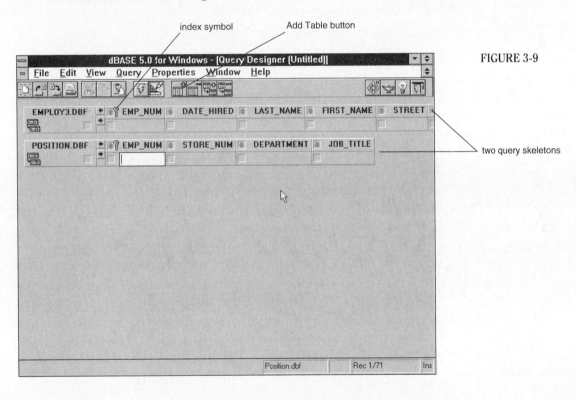

FIGURE 3-9

A query skeleton for the Position table is displayed below the Employ3 query skeleton. Both tables display ⚷ key symbols next to the EMP_NUM field name to show they are indexed on that field.

Because each table is a separate file, you need to tell dBASE how to link them.
To link the tables,

Choose: Query>Set Relation
or
Click: 🖳 Set Relation

> The Define Relations dialog
> box can also be opened by
> clicking 🖳 in the Employ3
> skeleton and dragging to the
> 🖳 in the Position skeleton.

The Define Relations dialog box is displayed. Since both the parent and child tables
have the same key fields, the dialog box displays the correct relationship. To accept
the link,

Choose: OK

Your screen should be similar to Figure 3-10.

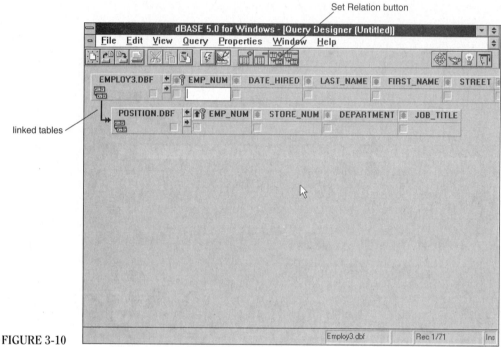

FIGURE 3-10

A line is drawn between the two table skeletons to show the tables are linked.

Finally, you need to specify the fields to be displayed in the view and enter the
date in the DATE_HIRED field. To do this,

> To move between table
> skeletons with the keyboard,
> use the [F3] Next and [F4]
> Previous keys.

- Place a check mark in the DATE_HIRED, LAST_NAME, FIRST_NAME,
  and DEPARTMENT fields selection check boxes.

- Enter the date condition <{1/1/91} in the DATE_HIRED condition field.

Run the query. The view displays the same 19 records, but now includes the DE-
PARTMENT field.

Your screen should be similar to Figure 3-11.

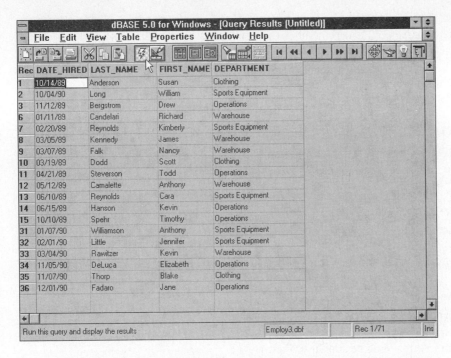

FIGURE 3-11

You feel the list would be more helpful if it was sorted by department. To make this change, switch back to the Query Designer.

The box to the left of each field name is the order box. It is used to specify the direction in which records are ordered in a query. The five order choices are:

Symbol	Order	Case
▦	Natural	
⬆	Ascending	insensitive
⬇	Descending	insensitive
⬆⬆	Ascending	sensitive
⬇⬇	Descending	sensitive

First you need to set EMP_NUM field in the Position table skeleton to natural order. To do this,

Move to: EMP_NUM field of Position table
Choose: ▦ Natural

To sort the query by department,

Move to: DEPARTMENT field
Choose: ⬆ Ascending

Run the query. The query is now sorted by department.

Querying for an Exact Match

Your next request is to look up a record for an employee who works in the Operations department. You remember the employee's name starts with a B but cannot remember the full name. You think you will recognize the name if you see it.

Instead of searching through the entire table, you can create a query that will find all the employees whose last names start with B and who work in the Operations department.

To remove the DATE_HIRED field from the query, switch to the Query Designer window, unmark the field's selection check box, and delete the date condition in the DATE condition field.

When querying for an exact match, you must enter the condition value exactly as you want dBASE to match. To find all employees whose last name starts with B,

Move to:	LAST_NAME condition field
Type:	**like "B*"**

To find an exact match for only the employee who works in the Operations department,

Move to:	DEPARTMENT condition field
Type:	**"Operations"**

Your screen should be similar to Figure 3-12.

FIGURE 3-12

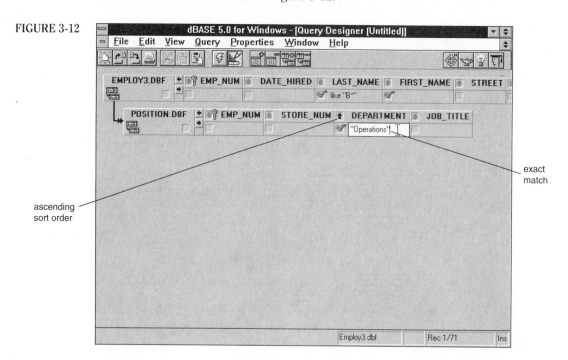

Run the query. The view displays the names of the two employees whose last name starts with B and who work in the Operations department. You now easily remember that the information was requested for Drew Bergstrom.

Querying Three Tables

The Regional Manager would like you to create some queries that will help in the analysis of employee payroll information. There is no payroll information in the tables you have used so far. The personnel department keeps that information in a dBASE table named Payrates. Switch to the Navigator window and open the Payrates table. This table contains the employee number and hourly pay rate and is already indexed on the EMP_NUM field.

The first query you want to create will find all the employees hired after November 15, 1992, and who work in the Clothing department. The Regional Manager would like the query to also display the employees' pay rates. The diagram below shows how the three tables are linked by the EMP_NUM field.

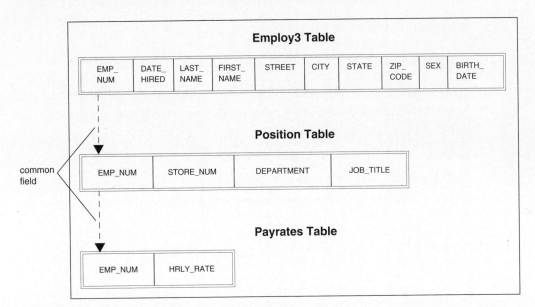

Switch to the Query Designer.
To add the Payrates table to the query skeleton,

Choose: Query>Add Table
➤ Ctrl + A
or
Choose: ⊞ Add Table
Choose: PAYRATES.DBF>OK

The three query table skeletons are displayed on the Query Designer window.
Next you need to link the Payrates table to the Position table by their common field, EMP_NUM. To do this,

Choose: Query>Set Relation
or
Click: ⊞ Set Relation
Choose: OK

> The Payrates table has already been indexed on the EMP_NUM field for you.

Next you will set up the conditions for the query.

■ To select only the records that have a hire date after 11/15/92, place a check mark in the DATE_HIRED selection check box and the condition >{11/15/92} in the condition field.

■ Clear the condition from the LAST_NAME condition field.

■ To select only the employees who work in the Clothing department, enter the condition "Clothing" in the DEPARTMENT condition field. Set the DEPARTMENT sort order back to Natural.

■ Finally, to display the HRLY_RATE, check the field's selection check box and change the sort order to Ascending. Change the sort order of the Payrates EMP_NUM field to Natural.

Your screen should be similar to Figure 3-13.

FIGURE 3-13

three linked tables

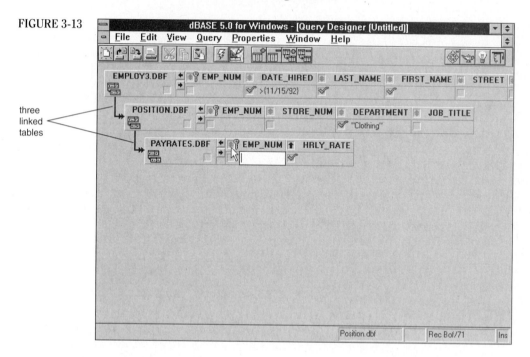

Run the query. The view shows that there are 11 employees who were hired after November 15, 1992, and who work in the Clothing department. Notice that the order of the fields displayed in the view is the same as the order of the opened tables in the Query Designer.

Creating a Calculated Field

The Regional Manager has also requested a list sorted by Department of all the employees who earn less than $5.50 per hour.

To create the query,

- Switch to the Query Designer window.

- Clear the check mark and condition from the DATE_HIRED field.

- Clear the condition from the DEPARTMENT field. Set the sort order to Ascending.

- Enter the condition <5.50 in the HRLY_RATE field. Set the sort order to Natural.

Your screen should be similar to Figure 3-14.

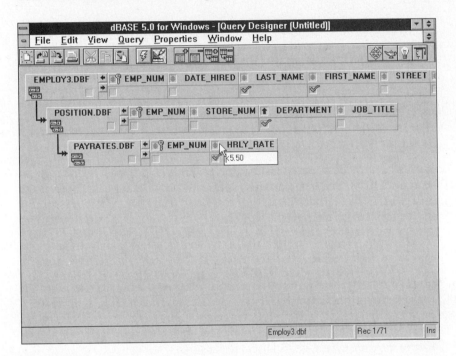

FIGURE 3-14

Run the query.

The Regional Manager reviewed the list of employees who earn less than $5.50 and has decided it is time to give these employees a raise. He would like you to create a query that will calculate a 5 percent increase for these employees.

To do this, you will create a calculated field. A **calculated field** contains values calculated from one or more other fields. Calculated fields generally should not be included in the table design structure because they take up space and can easily be created as needed.

Switch to the Query Designer.

To create a calculated field,

Choose: Query>Create Calculated Field

Your screen should be similar to Figure 3-15.

default field
name

calculated
field
skeleton

calculated
field entry
area

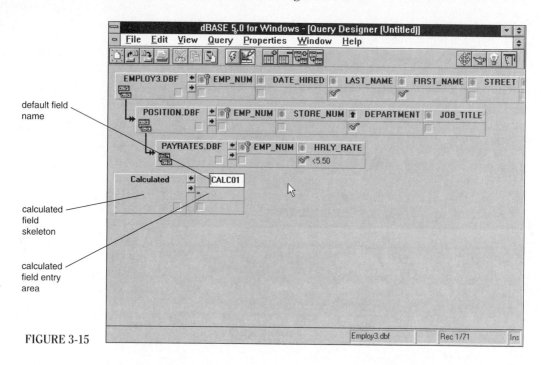

FIGURE 3-15

A blank calculated field skeleton is displayed. It displays a default field name of CALC01. You want to replace the default field name with a more descriptive name for the new field.

Select the CALC01 field name.

Type: **NEW_RATE**

Next you need to enter the formula to calculate the pay raise. The formula will multiply the value in the HRLY_RATE field by 1.05 to calculate the 5 percent increase for each employee. The formula is entered following the = sign in the calculated field entry area.

Move to the calculated field condition field space.

Type: **HRLY_RATE*1.05**

Mark the calculated field check box.

Note: If the formula is highlighted in yellow and the error message "Variable undefined HRLY_RATE" appears in the status line, you need to clarify the location of the HRLY_RATE field. To do this, switch to the Payrates table, then switch back to the Query Designer window. To clear the yellow highlight, press ⬆, then ⬇.

Field names can be entered in uppercase or lowercase characters because they are not case sensitive.

The field that is used in the calculated field condition must be checked or the table that contains the field must be open.

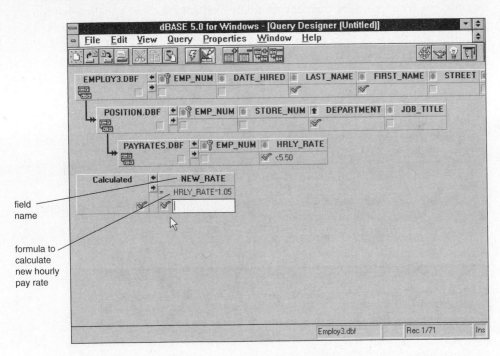

field name

formula to calculate new hourly pay rate

FIGURE 3-16

Run the query. The New Rate column displays the calculated values.

Use the Print command on the File menu to print the view.

The last query the Regional Manager requested will display the weekly gross pay for all employees. To calculate the weekly gross pay, you will need to use the table Hours, which contains the employee number, week ending date, and hours worked in the week.

Open the Hours table. The Hours table contains the number of hours worked by each employee during different weekly periods. The same employee number is used multiple times.

Switch to the Query Designer window.

Choose:	Query>Add Table
or	
Click:	Add Table
Choose:	HOURS.DBF>OK

Link the EMP_NUM field of the Payrates table with the Hours table.

When you link tables, you create a relationship between them. This relationship can be a single-valued relationship or a multivalued relationship. A **single-valued relationship** exists if every record in one table is related to only one (or none) of the records in the other table. This is the situation with the relationship between the first three tables in the query skeleton. It can also exist when many records in the parent table are related to only one record in the child table. These relationships are also called one-to-one and many-to-one.

A **multivalued relationship** exists if every record in one table is related to no records, one record, or more than one record in another table. This is the relationship that exists between the parent table and the Hours table. For every one employee record in the Employ3 table, there are several records related to that employee in the Hours table. This type of relationship is also called one-to-many.

To enter the query condition,

■   Enter the condition {10/20/95} in the END_DATE condition field.

■   Clear the condition from the HRLY_RATE field.

■   Clear the check mark from the DEPARTMENT field and return the sort order to Natural.

■   Change the calculated field name to GROSS_PAY.

To calculate the gross pay for the employees, move to the calculated field condition area. Revise the formula to be: HRLY_RATE*HOURS

Your screen should be similar to Figure 3-17.

FIGURE 3-17

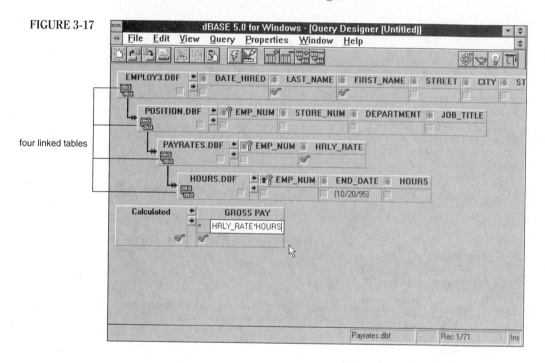

Run the query. The view displays the gross pay for each employee for the week of October 20, 1995, in a new column.

You anticipate that the Regional Manager will request this report frequently, so you would like to save the query to use again to quickly produce another report. Switch back to the Query Design window and use the Save As command on the File menu to save the query settings as GROSSPAY.

The query file is saved with a .QBE file extension.

Note: If you are running short on lab time, this is an appropriate place to end the session. When you begin again, load dBASE and open the GROSSPAY query.

Creating a Multitable Form

You have been using several tables of employee information that need to be updated each time information changes in an existing record. The form you created to use with the Employ2 table can only update the records in that table. You want to create a form that will update the Employ3, Payrates, and Position tables. To do this, you create a query of the fields you want to update and then create a form based on the query.

To modify the GROSSPAY query, you need to remove the Hours table and the calculated field from the Query Designer window.

Move to any field in the Hours table skeleton.

To remove the table from the window,

Choose: Query>Remove Selected Table
or
Click: ⊞ Remove Table

The Hours table is no longer displayed in the Query Designer window.

In a similar manner, remove the calculated field skeleton from the Query Designer window.

You would like to include all the fields in the three tables in the query.

Select all the fields in the Employ3, Position, and Payrates table skeletons.

Next, you need to remove the checks from the duplicate EMP_NUM fields so the employee number appears only once in the view.

Unmark the EMP_NUM field in the Position and Payrates table skeletons. Finally, you need to clear the check mark from the LAST_NAME+ Employ3–>FIRST_NAME field in the Employ3 table skeleton. (This field was created automatically by dBASE when the First and Last Name index was created.) Unmark the LAST_NAME+Employ3–>FIRST_NAME field in the Employ3 table skeleton.

Run the Query. All fields from the three tables are included in the view, and the Emp_Num field appears only once.

Return to the Query Designer window and use the Save As command to save the query as UPDATE. Close the Query Designer window and the Hours and Payrates tables.

To create a form from the UPDATE query,

Choose: File>New
or
Click: ▣ New
Choose: Form

> To quickly select all the fields in a table skeleton, select the check box below the table name.

The Form Expert dialog box is displayed. To use Expert Assistance to create the form,

Choose: Next

> You can also select "Untitled" from the Forms group in the Navigator window to create a new form.

To select the query to use for the form, from the Available Files list,

Choose: UPDATE.QBE>Next

DATABASE

Your screen should be similar to Figure 3-18.

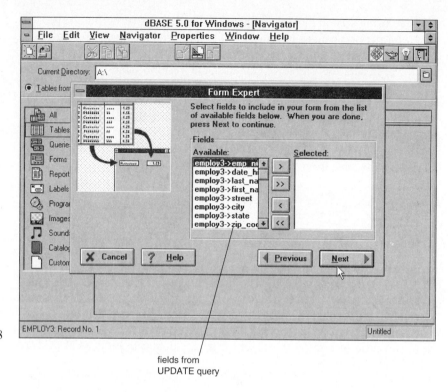

FIGURE 3-18

fields from
UPDATE query

The fields from the three tables are listed in the Available list box.

Next you need to select the fields in the order you want the data entered on the form. Select the fields in the following order:

FIRST_NAME
LAST_NAME
STREET
CITY
STATE
ZIP_CODE
SEX
BIRTH_DATE
EMP_NUM
DATE_HIRED
STORE_NUM
DEPARTMENT
JOB_TITLE
HRLY_RATE

Your screen should be similar to Figure 3-19.

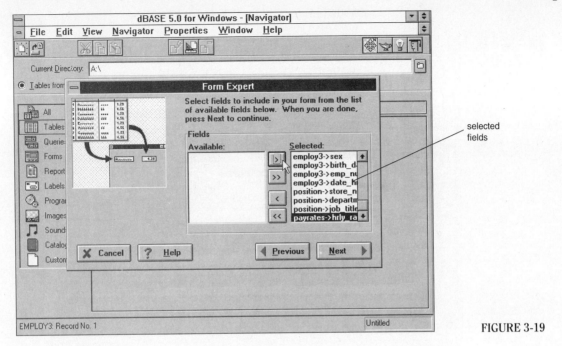

FIGURE 3-19

Choose: Next

The default columnar layout is acceptable for this form.

Choose: Next

This dialog box allows you to change the font size and color of the objects on the form.

Fonts consist of typefaces and size. The **typeface** is the appearance and shape of characters in a font. Common typefaces are Roman and Courier. **Size** refers to the size of the printed characters, commonly measured in points. A point is about 1/72 inch in height. A common point size is 12. This means the printed character is about 12/72 inch in height. Additionally, you can change the **attributes** of type, such as bold, italics, and underlines.

The Font section of the dialog box is used to specify the font for the form title, text, or entries. You would like to increase the size of the text from 8 points to 10 points so it is easier to read. To do this,

Choose: Fonts

From the Fonts area of the dialog box, you need to select the Text ✍ Tool button.

Choose: ✍ Tool (on the Text line)

Click on ✍ Tool or use Tab ⇆
to move to the button and
press ⏎ Enter.

DATABASE

Your screen should be similar to Figure 3-20.

FIGURE 3-20

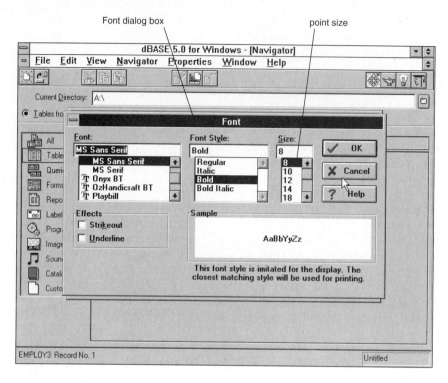

The Font dialog box is displayed. To change the size of the text,

Choose: Size>10

The Sample text box displays an example of the text in the larger point size.

Choose: OK

The previous Form Expert dialog box is displayed again. In addition, you want to change the background color of the form.

Choose: Background Color

You can also open the Form drop-down list box to display a color list.

Press ↓ to cycle from one color to the next.
     The sample box shows the selected color.
     Select a color of your choice.

Do not select yellow or you will be unable to read the form title.

Choose: Create

Your screen should be similar to Figure 3-21.

form in
column layout

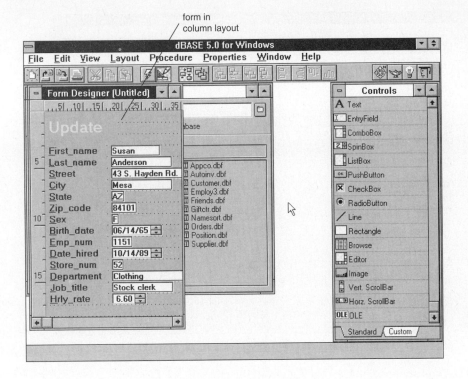

FIGURE 3-21

The Form Designer window displays the form in the column layout. You will use this window to refine the layout of the form.

Maximize the Form Designer window. Rearrange the objects in the form as in Figure 3-22 on the next page. Add the titles PERSONAL DATA and COMPANY DATA by inserting text objects on the form in the locations shown in Figure 3-22. Modify the form title to be Employee Data Entry Form.

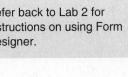

Refer back to Lab 2 for instructions on using Form Designer.

DATABASE

Your screen should be similar to Figure 3-22.

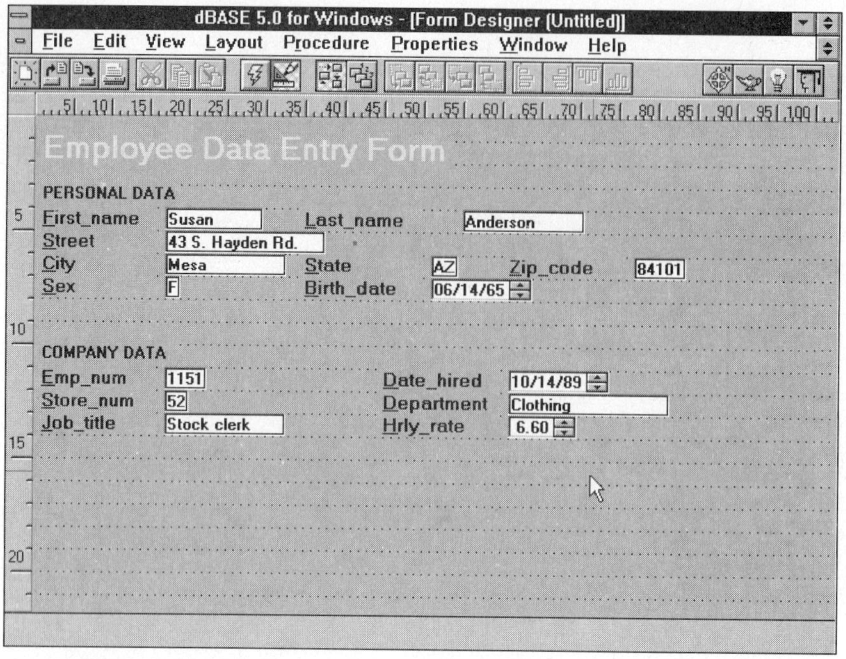

FIGURE 3-22

When you are done, to view the data from the tables in the form,

Choose: View>Form
or
Click: 🔩 Run Form

The Save Form dialog box is displayed. Name the form UPDATE. Use the Find Records command to quickly display the record containing your information.

To see how quickly the form can be used to update all three files, you will make several changes in the data.

Change your zip code to 85000, the store number to 68, and your hourly rate to 9.75.

Print the form with your record information displayed. Close the Form Designer.

To verify that the changes were made to the tables, open each of the tables, locate your record, and note the changes.

As you can see, using a single customized form to update records in all three tables simultaneously is a great time-saving feature.

Close all the open tables. Exit dBASE. Exit Windows.

Key Terms

query   (DB90)
query by example   (DB90)
QBE   (DB90)
view   (DB90)
skeleton   (DB91)
field selection check box   (DB91)
condition field   (DB91)
operator   (DB95)
reserved word   (DB95)
wildcard operator   (DB95)
comparison operator   (DB97)
relational operator   (DB97)
logical AND   (DB98)

logical OR   (DB98)
link   (DB101)
multitable query   (DB101)
parent table   (DB101)
child table   (DB101)
calculated field   (DB109)
single-valued relationship   (DB111)
multivalued relationship   (DB112)
font   (DB115)
typeface   (DB115)
size   (DB115)
attribute   (DB115)

Command Summary

Command	Shortcut	SpeedBar	Action
File>New>Query			Opens Query Designer
View>Query Results	F2		Displays results of a query
View>Query Design	⇧ Shift + F2		Displays design of a query
Window>1 Navigator			Switches to Navigator window
Query>Add Table	Ctrl + A		Adds table to query
Query>Set Relation			Defines relation between tables
Query>Create Calculated Field			Inserts a calculated field
Query>Remove Selected Table			Removes selected table from query

LAB REVIEW

Matching

1. >
2. view
3. query
4. logical OR
5. query skeleton
6. index field
7. calculated field
8. Like
9. Set Relations
10. child table

_____ **a.** special operator to find all similar values

_____ **b.** represents fields of a table

_____ **c.** used to link queries

_____ **d.** greater-than comparison operator

_____ **e.** field created from values in one or more fields

_____ **f.** temporary window that displays output of a query

_____ **g.** table you are linking to

_____ **h.** multiple-condition query

_____ **i.** window used to ask questions about database tables

_____ **j.** used to link query fields together

Practice Exercises

1. To complete this problem, you must have completed the tables in Practice Exercise 2 of Lab 1 and Exercise 4 of Lab 2. Pam would like to create some reports from the data in the Travel Abroad tables.

   a. Open the table Staff. Open the table Trips. Index the tables on EMP_NUM. Close the tables.

   b. Create a query that displays the employee names and the destinations of the trips that they sold. Print the query.

   c. Create a query that displays the EMP_NUM, TICKET_NUM, TRIP_DEST, and TRAV_DATE. Print the query.

   d. Create a query that displays the EMP_NUM, FIRST_NAME, LAST_NAME, and DATE_HIRED for the employees hired before 10/1/94. Print the query.

2. Anthony owns the Office Supply Warehouse, which has grown rapidly over the last year. He wants to replace his manual system of customer records with a computerized database. He hopes this new system will make it easier to bill his customers in a timely manner. Anthony has created several tables already, but he needs some help and has hired you as a consultant to finish setting up the database.

   a. Open the table Customer. Open the table Orders. Modify the table structures to make the common field the index field in both tables.

   b. Enter your name in the Customer table as a new record. Include a customer number in the record. The address can be fictitious.

   c. Add the same customer number to the Order table with a order number of 845, quantity of 1000, and a description as Letterhead paper. Enter the current date in the Date column.

orders

   d. Close the tables. Create a query that displays the customers' names who
       have order dates before 6/5/95 OR a quantity greater than 500. Print the
       query.

   e. Create a query that displays the customer names, order number, quan-
       tity, and description.

   f. If you have a mouse, move the columns in the order: Order Number,
       Customer Name, Description, and Quantity.

   g. Print the query.

   h. Create a custom form with a layout of your choice that will update both
       tables. Enhance the form. Print the form displaying your record.

3. To complete this problem, you must have completed Practice Exercise 3 in
Lab 2. As inventory control manager of The Gift Center, you would like to create
some queries to display the information stored in the Gifts and Supplier tables.

   a. Open the table Gifts. Open the table Supplier. Modify the table structures
       to make the common field the index field in both tables. Close the tables.

   b. Create a query using the Gifts and Supplier tables that displays all the
       products supplied by Wilson Distributors with a discount price of more
       than $35.00. Print the query.

   c. Create a query that displays the price and discount price of all the gifts
       with a discount price of less than $50.00 and supplied by Jackson Suppliers.
       Create a calculated field that will increase the discount price of the items
       by 7 percent. Print the query.

   d. Create a query that displays the item number, description, supplier's
       name, and price of the products with a price of more than $75.00.

   e. If you have a mouse, move the columns in the order: Item Number,
       Description, Supplier Name, and Price.

   f. Save the query as Sales. Print the query.

4. Rebecca owns a small photo framing business. She wants to keep track of her
inventory using dBASE. Her inventory includes such items as premade frames,
custom frames, children's frames, mat board, glass, cardboard and so on.

   a. Create a table to hold the item number, item name, and retail price of
       each item that is kept in inventory. Name the table Photoinv.

   b. Create a table to hold the item number, order quantity, reorder point
       quantity, and quantity on hand. Name the table Photoqty.

   c. Enter at least 15 items into each of the tables. Enter your name as the
       last item in the inventory table. Be sure to use the same item numbers
       in both tables.

   d. Create a query that shows each of the items in inventory along with the
       quantity on hand and the reorder point. Print the query.

   e. Create a second query that shows the item, quantity on hand, order
       quantity, and reorder point quantity. Print the query.

DATABASE

5. Create a database for a company of your choice. Create at least three tables and enter a minimum of 10 records in each table. Include numeric data such as quantity, price, or salary in at least one table. Create a simple query of the database using multiple tables. Create a query that calculates a new field. Print the queries. Enter your name and the current date in one of the fields that is displayed in the queries.

4 Reporting Data Using Crystal Reports

CASE STUDY

The Regional Manager is impressed with your ability to use dBASE to quickly locate and analyze the data in the employee tables. You have used the program to automate the daily updates and changes that occur to the employee tables and to quickly find answers to many different types of queries. The last major task you need to do is create weekly and monthly employee status reports.

As you organized the employee database, different tables were created to hold different types of information on the employees. You have used these tables in multitable queries. Now you will use them to produce several different reports.

Note: You must have a mouse connected to your system to complete this lab.

Designing a Report

Load Windows. Put your data disk in drive A (or the appropriate drive for your system). Load dBASE for Windows. If necessary, change the current directory to the drive containing your data disk.

You have already used dBASE to create and print several simple reports using the Print command on the File menu. Reports are the output you generate from queries or tables.

Competencies

After completing this lab, you will know how to:

1. Design a report.
2. Preview a report.
3. Edit text fields.
4. Add text fields.
5. Align objects.
6. Sort a report.
7. Create a multitable report.
8. Group a report.
9. Enhance a report.
10. Create totals.
11. Change margins.
12. Create a catalog.

DATABASE

The Regional Manager would like a report that displays the employees' names and addresses ordered by employee number. dBASE comes with a separate report program called **Crystal Reports**. Crystal Reports is a powerful program for creating custom reports, lists, and form letters using data from existing dBASE tables. To use the Crystal Report feature to display the data in the Employ3 table,

Choose: File>New>Report>EMPLOY3.DBF>OK

or

Click: ▣ >Report>EMPLOY3.DBF>OK

The Crystal Report welcome screen is displayed. After a few seconds, the Crystal Reports for dBASE window is displayed.

Your screen should be similar to Figure 4-1.

You can also choose Reports from the Navigator and then select Untitled to create a new report.

FIGURE 4-1

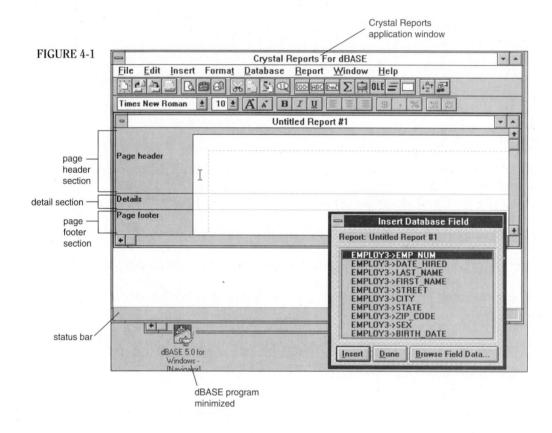

Notice the dBASE 5.0 for Windows icon in the lower left corner of the window. When Crystal Reports is running, the dBASE program is minimized. This is because Crystal Reports is a separate application program.

The Crystal Reports window contains a menu, two SpeedBars, and a status bar that work the same as in the dBASE program. The SpeedBar tools available for use in the Crystal Reports window are identified below.

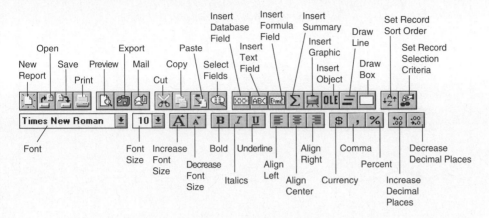

Inside the Crystal Reports window, the Report window is open. This window displays the **Report Designer**, which is used to control the layout of your report. You choose the fields from the table or query to appear in the report and rearrange the information in any way you want. You can customize the report design to meet your needs by adding, deleting, and defining different report features. For example, you can group related data together, perform arithmetic operations to display such information as totals and subtotals, and create headers, footers, and page numbers on each page. Additionally, you can add graphic elements such as lines, boxes, and pictures.

The Report Designer is divided horizontally into three sections. The sections are identified by section names on the left side of the window. The white space next to the section name is where you enter the information you want to appear in each section. Initially the Report Design contains three types of sections:

Page header	Contains information to be printed at the top of each page as a page header
Details	Contains the records of the table
Page footer	Contains information to be printed at the bottom of each page as a page footer

The Insert Database Field dialog box is also open. This dialog box lists the field names from the Employ3 table. You use this dialog box to specify the fields of data to be included in the report.

The first report you have been asked to create will display the following information.

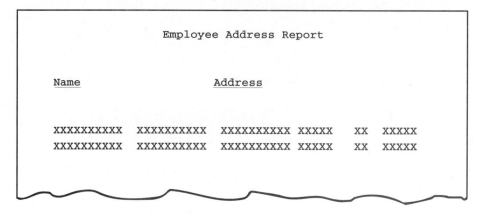

The first step in creating a report is to select the fields from the dialog box that you want to add to the details section of the report. The first field you want to add is the FIRST_NAME field. To do this,

The file name precedes the field name in the dialog box.

| **Select:** | FIRST_NAME |
| **Choose:** | **I**nsert |

Notice that the mouse pointer changes to a ⌷. This indicates you can use the mouse to position the field in the Report Designer.

You can also double-click the field name to both select it and choose Insert.

To position the field at the left margin, move the mouse pointer until the box is displayed next to the left margin in the details section. Then, to place the field, click the left mouse button.

Your screen should be similar to Figure 4-2.

FIGURE 4-2

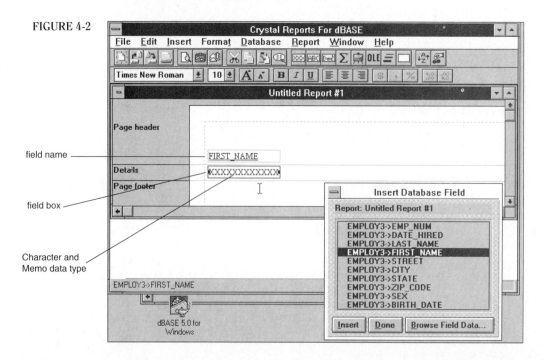

The field name is displayed in the page header section, and a rectangular field box is displayed in the details section. The field name is displayed in all capital letters and is underlined. The field box represents the size, position, and data type of the inserted field. The **data type** is a classification of the data that appears in the field. The characters displayed in the field box represent the data type the field contains, as follows:

Characters	Data Type
XXXXX	Character and Memo
555,555	Numeric and Float
YYYY–MM_DD	Date
YES/NO	Logical

The 12 X's in the FIRST_NAME field box indicate it is a Character data type and is 12 character spaces wide.

Next you want to insert the LAST_NAME field into the report. Another way to insert fields is to drag them from the Insert Database Field dialog box to the report. To insert the LAST_NAME field,

Select: LAST_NAME

Drag the mouse pointer until it is positioned just to the right of the FIRST_NAME field in the details section.

The rest of the fields you want to add to this report are grouped together in the Insert Database Field dialog box. Instead of adding each field individually, you can select multiple fields and add them all at the same time. To do this,

Select: STREET

While holding down the ⟨⇧Shift⟩ + ⟨Ctrl⟩ keys,

Select: ZIP_CODE

If you insert the wrong field in the report, click on the field box to select it. When a blue border is displayed, press ⟨Delete⟩. Delete the field name in a similar manner.

Holding down ⟨Ctrl⟩ alone will select multiple fields independently.

DATABASE

Your screen should be similar to Figure 4-3.

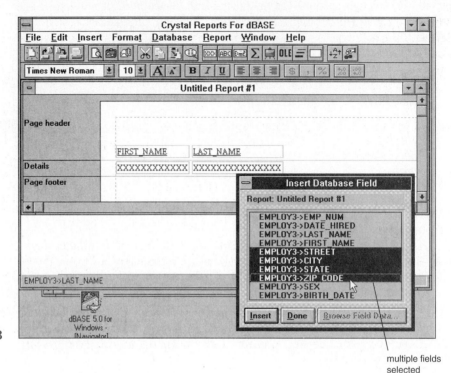

multiple fields
selected

FIGURE 4-3

All fields between and including the first and last selected fields are selected.

Using either placement method, place the selected fields immediately to the right of the LAST_NAME field on the details section of the report.

When multiple fields are selected and added to the report, the fields are placed in the details section in the order they are displayed in the Insert Database Fields dialog box. If you try to add more fields to the report than there is space in the report width, any fields that do not fit are not added.

Now that all the fields are added to the report, you would like to close the Insert Database Field dialog box. To do this,

Choose: **D**one

The dialog box is closed.

To see the CITY, STATE and ZIP_CODE fields, use the scroll bar to scroll the Report window. To see more of the records in the window, maximize the Report window.

You can quickly scroll the window by dragging the scroll box to the right.

Your screen should be similar to Figure 4-4.

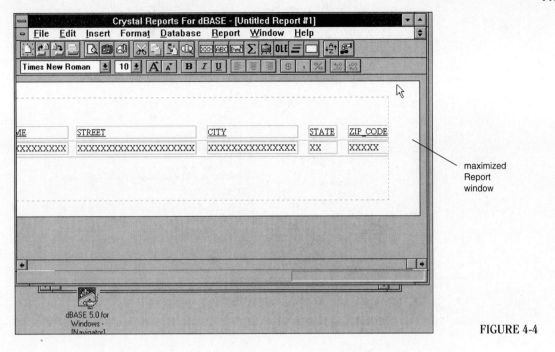

maximized
Report
window

FIGURE 4-4

Now that all the fields are placed on the report, you would like to see how the report will look.

Previewing the Report

You can view how the report will appear when printed by using the File menu or the 🔍 Preview button. To preview the report,

Choose: **F**ile>**P**rint>**W**indow
or
Click: 🔍 Preview

As Crystal Reports is preparing your report, it displays the number of records being read and sorted and the percentage of the total that have already been processed in the status bar of the Preview window. After a few moments, the report is generated and displayed in the Preview window.

Your screen should be similar to Figure 4-5.

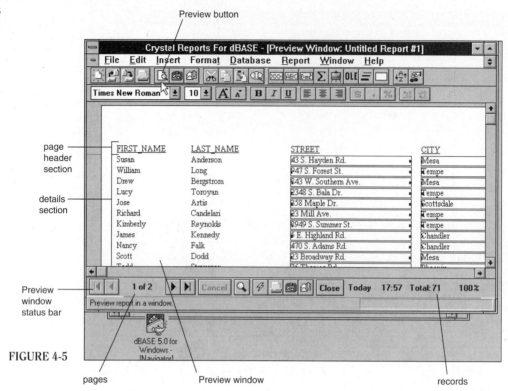

Preview button

page header section

details section

Preview window status bar

FIGURE 4-5

pages

Preview window

records

The information in the page header section of the Report Designer controls the information that is displayed as a header at the top of each page of the report, in this case, the field names. The database field boxes in the details section control which fields of data from the table are displayed in the body of the report.

The bottom of the Preview window contains a status bar that displays information about the report and contains buttons that can be used in the Preview window. The status bar information tells you that you are viewing page 1 of 2 of the report and that there are 71 records displayed. The status bar buttons are identified below.

Button	Keyboard Equivalent	Action
◀◀	Ctrl + Home	Returns to first page of report
◀	Page Up	Returns to previous page of report
▶	Page Down	Moves to next page of report
▶▶	Ctrl + End	Moves to last page of report
Cancel		Stops running report
🔍		Shows three different magnifications of report
⚡		Rereads data in database
🖨		Prints report
📧		Exports report to a file
📧		Exports report to e-mail
Close		Closes the Preview window

View the second page of the report. Use the horizontal scroll bar to display the report fields to the right.

To close the Preview window,

Choose: Close

You are returned to the Report window. After looking at the preview of the report, you would like to make some changes to it before printing it.

> If there are blue borders surrounding the fields of data, this is because these fields are still selected in the Report Designer.

Editing Text Fields

First you would like to edit the column headings in the report. The field names from the table were used as the column headings and entered as text fields in the report. Like a form, the different parts of a report are objects that can be selected and modified. You would like to change the column heading FIRST_NAME to Name.

Select the FIRST_NAME field name.

The field name is displayed with a blue editing border and handles, indicating it is selected. The name of the selected field appears in the status bar. To change the name,

Choose: Edit>Text Field

Your screen should be similar to Figure 4-6.

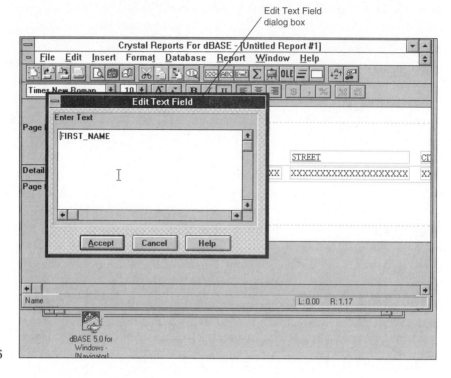

FIGURE 4-6

The Edit Text Field dialog box is displayed. To edit text, you can use the editing features you learned in Lab 1 or delete the existing text and replace it with new text.
Change the column heading to Name.
To accept the changes,

Choose: Accept

You cannot choose Accept by pressing ←Enter.

The field name is changed to Name. Changing the field name in the report does not affect the field name in the underlying table.
Next you would like to change the STREET field name to Address. The Edit Text Field command is also on the SpeedMenu.
Right-click on the STREET field name.
From the SpeedMenu,

Choose: Edit Text Field

Change the field name to Address.
To accept the name change,

Choose: Accept

You no longer want the field name LAST_NAME displayed in the report. To delete a field name, you select it and press Delete.
Delete the LAST_NAME field name.

Your screen should be similar to Figure 4-7.

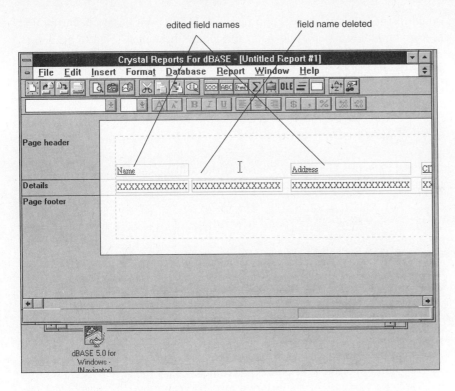

FIGURE 4-7

In a similar manner, delete the CITY, STATE and ZIP_CODE field names.

You would like to see how the changes you made affect the report. To preview the report,

Choose: **F**ile>**P**rint>**W**indow

or

Click: Preview

The Saved Data dialog box is displayed. You can use the saved data or refresh the data in the database before previewing the report. Since you are the only user of this database table and you have not made any changes to the database, you can use the saved data.

Choose: Use **S**aved Data

Use the scroll bars and page buttons to view the entire report.

After looking at the report, you decide to adjust the spacing on the report so that there is a blank line below the column headings. Additionally, you want to add a report title.

Close the Preview window.

You can select multiple objects in the Report Designer by holding down Ctrl while clicking on the object.

DATABASE

Adding Text Fields

You would like to separate the column headings in the page header from the first detail record by adding a blank line below the column headings. To add a blank line, you need to display the insertion point before the Name heading.

Move the mouse pointer before the Name heading. When the mouse pointer is displayed as an I-beam I, click the mouse button.

Then, to add a blank line,

Press: ←Enter

Next you would like to add a title to the report that will appear as a header at the top of each page. To add a report title to the page header section,

Choose: Insert>Text Field
or
Click: Insert Text Field

The Edit Text Field dialog box is displayed. To enter the text,

Type: **Employee Address Report**
Choose: Accept

The mouse pointer appears with a field placeholder box. Crystal Reports is waiting for you to select a location for the inserted text. You can move the placeholder box anywhere in the report using the mouse.

Move the placeholder box until it is displayed at the left margin on the first line of the page header section of the report. Click the mouse button. If necessary, increase the size of the text box to fully display the title by dragging the right border sizing handle.

Your screen should be similar to Figure 4-8.

FIGURE 4-8

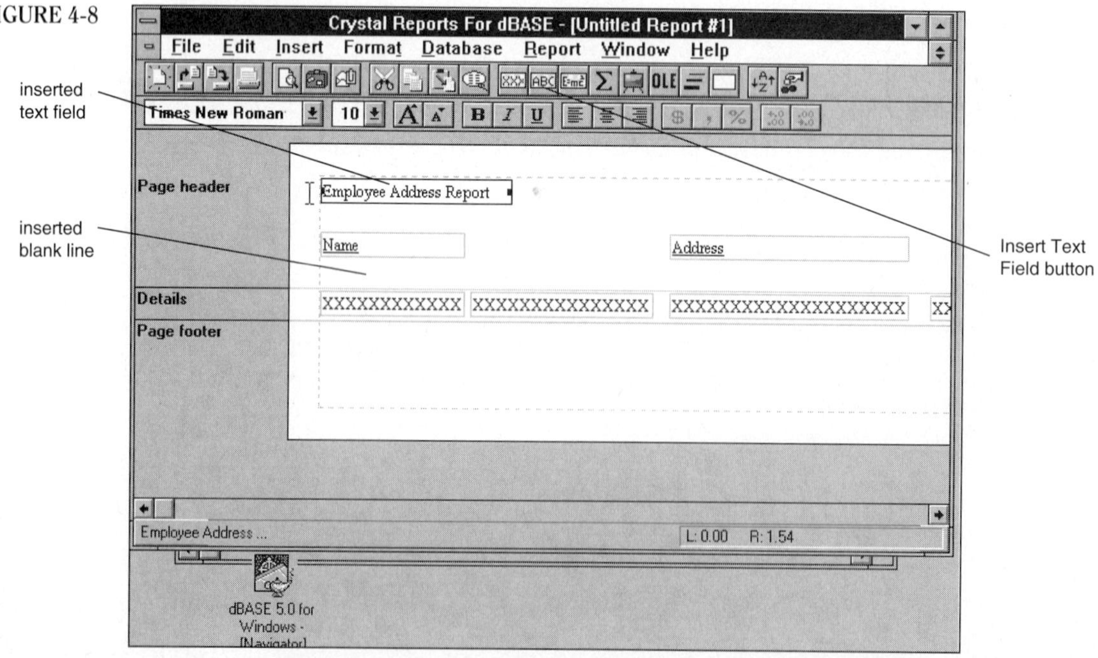

The text is inserted into the placeholder box at the selected location.

You will further improve the report by enhancing the appearance of the title by changing the font settings and attributes associated with the text. To enlarge the title and make it appear bold,

Choose: Forma**t**>**F**ont

Your screen should be similar to Figure 4-9.

You can also use the
Change Font command on
the SpeedMenu.

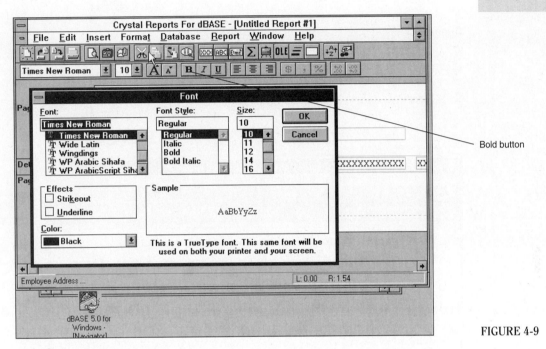

FIGURE 4-9

The current font and style settings for the selected object are displayed in the Font dialog box. The current font is Times New Roman, with regular style settings in 10-point type size. To change the type size of the title,

Choose: **S**ize>14

The Sample box shows an example of how text will appear in the new size setting. You would also like the title displayed in bold. To do this,

Choose: Font St**y**le>Bold

You can also use the
SpeedBar buttons to make
these font and style changes.

The Sample box again changes to reflect your selection.

Choose: OK

The Font dialog box is closed and the title is displayed in bold and in a larger point size. The lower SpeedBar shows that the text in the currently selected object is 14 points. Additionally, the ▣ Bold button appears depressed, indicating this selection is on.

Aligning Objects

You would like the report title centered over the report. To do this, you use the Alignment command to align the text within the box. To center the text between the left and right margins, you must increase the size of the text box surrounding the title so it extends across the width of the page.

To expand the size of the box, point to the right border sizing handle. Drag the outline until you reach the right margin of the report. Release the mouse button.

Then, to center the text,

> The dashed line displayed on the Report window marks the margins for the report.

Choose: Format>Field>Alignment>Centered>OK
or
Click: ▤ Align Center

Your screen should be similar to Figure 4-10.

FIGURE 4-10

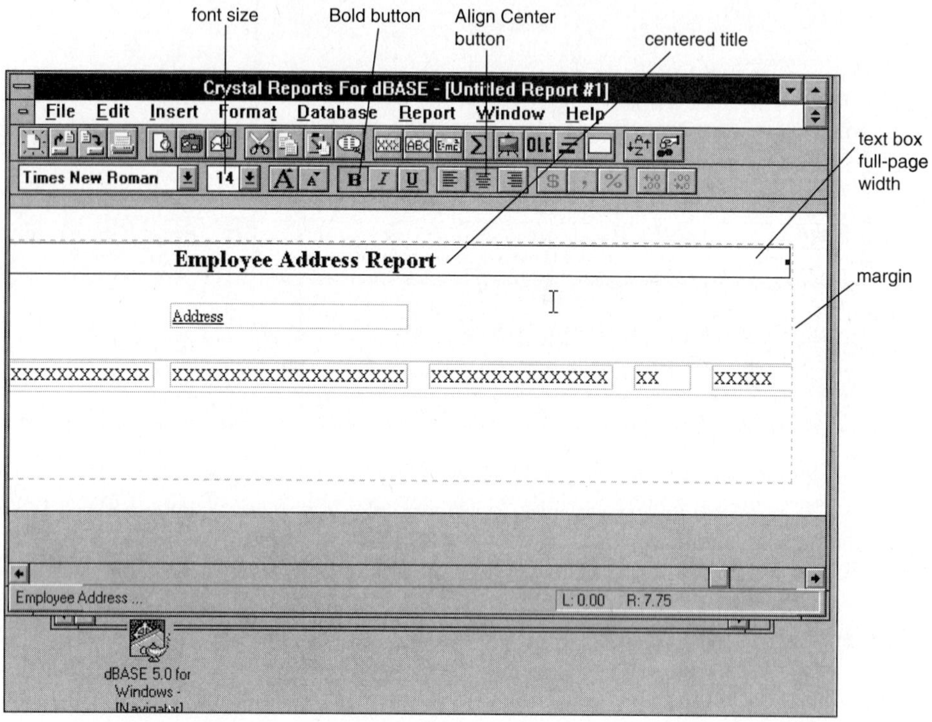

The report heading is centered in the box.

Sorting the Report

The last thing you need to do to this report is set the sort order for the report. The Regional Manager would like the report sorted by the employees' last names. To do this,

Choose: **R**eport>Record **S**ort Order
or
Click: 🔢 Sort Order
Select: LAST_NAME
Choose: **A**dd-->
Choose: OK

To see how the changes you have made affect the report, preview the report.

You would like to be able to see the entire width of the page on the screen. To do this, you use the Magnify button on the status bar.

Click: 🔍 Magnify

Your screen should be similar to Figure 4-11.

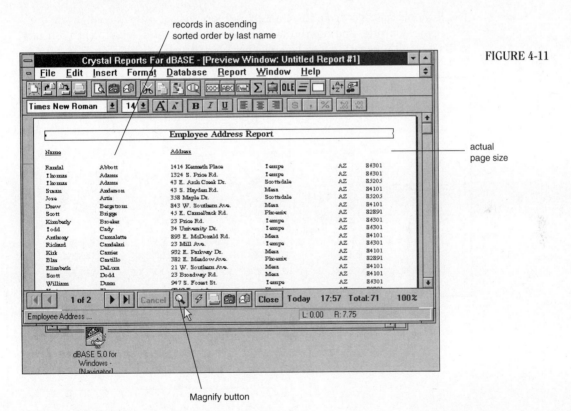

records in ascending
sorted order by last name

FIGURE 4-11

actual
page size

Magnify button

The report is displayed in actual page size, just as it will appear when printed. The records appear in ascending alphabetical order by last name.

To see a full page of the report in the Preview window,

Click: 🔍 Magnify

The entire first page is displayed, reduced in size to fit in the Preview window.

You could make other changes to this report; however, you are satisfied with the report as it is and want to print the report. To do this,

> You can resize the Preview window, and the page image will be resized as well.

Choose: <u>F</u>ile><u>P</u>rint><u>P</u>rinter
or
Click: 🖨 Print
Choose: OK

> Reports are saved with a .RPT file extension.

Use the Save As command on the File menu to save the report as EMPLIST. Close the Preview window and exit the Crystal Report program.

The dBASE program is maximized and you are returned to the Navigator window.

Creating a Multitable Report

The Regional Manager would like another report that displays the employee number, name, job title, and hourly rate, grouped by store and department. You have sketched out the report to look like the one shown below.

```
                        Monthly Employee Report
                                Date

                   NUMBER    NAME                 JOB TITLE  PAY RATE

Store Number:   XX

  Department:   XXXXXXXX

                   XXX       XXXXXXXX XXXXXXX      XXXXX      XXXXX
                   XXX       XXXXXXXX XXXXXXX      XXXXX      XXXXX
```

Because this report contains data from the Employ3, Position, and Payrate tables, before you can create the report you must create a query that contains the fields. To create a query for the report,

Choose: Eile>New>Query
or
Click: 🖼 New File>Query

The Open Table Required dialog box is displayed. To make the Employ3 table the parent table in the query,

Choose: Employ3>OK

Maximize the Query Designer window. Add the Position and Payrates tables to the Query Designer window. Link the tables on the EMP_NUM field.

Your screen should be similar to Figure 4-12.

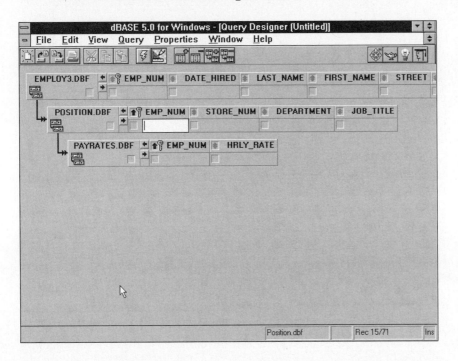

FIGURE 4-12

You can choose Queries from the Navigator and then select Untitled to open a new query.

It is not necessary to select any fields in the Query Designer. When none are selected, all fields will be listed in the Insert Database Fields dialog box when you create a new report.

Save the query as PAYRATES.

To create a new report,

Choose: Eile>New>Report
or
Click: 🖼 New File>Report

DATABASE

The Report Designer window is displayed. Because the query is still open in dBASE, Crystal Reports does not prompt you for a table to base the report on. Maximize the Report window.

Next you need to select the fields you want in the report.

Add the EMP_NUM, FIRST_NAME, LAST_NAME, JOB_TITLE, and HRLY_RATE fields to the Report Designer. Then choose Done.

Your screen should be similar to Figure 4-13.

FIGURE 4-13

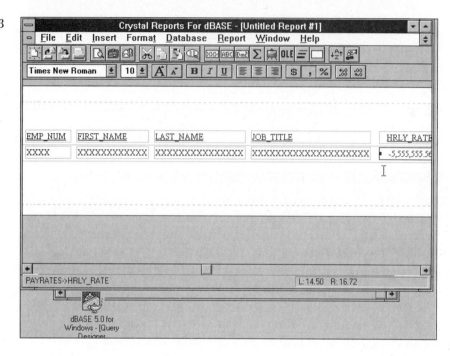

To preview how the report will appear when printed,

Choose: File>Print>Window

or

Click: 🔍 Preview

After a few moments, the report is generated and displayed in the Preview window. View both pages of the report using the Magnify button as needed. When you are done, close the Preview window.

Grouping the Report

After looking over the report, you decide it would be more meaningful if the employees were grouped by store number. **Grouping** is one of the most powerful features of the Report Designer. Grouping lets you organize and arrange the data for clarity and ease of understanding.

To change the report design to group the data by store, you need to add and define a group section.

Choose: Insert>Group Section

The Insert Group Section dialog box is displayed. To specify the field that you want the report grouped on, from the top list box,

Choose: POSITION.DBF-->STORE_NUM

The program will first sort the report data on the STORE_NUM field and then it will group the data in the report whenever the store number changes.

The bottom list box shows that the default sort order is ascending order. This order is acceptable for this report. To close the dialog box,

Choose: OK

If necessary, scroll the window to see the section names.
Your screen should be similar to Figure 4-14.

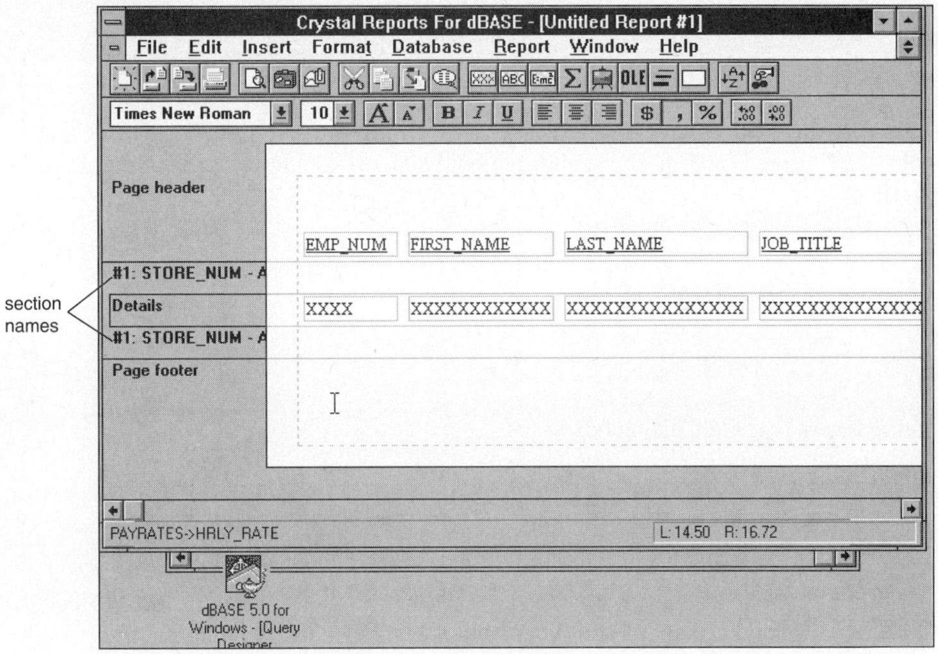

FIGURE 4-14

The Report Designer displays a new group section above and below the details section.
Preview the report. Use the Magnify button to view the full report page.

Your screen should be similar to Figure 4-15.

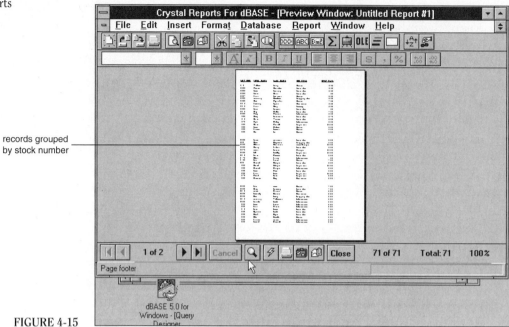

records grouped
by stock number

FIGURE 4-15

Although the records are grouped, you cannot identify which group is associated with each store. To clarify the report, you will add a text field to describe the group section.

Close the Preview window.

Choose: **I**nsert>Te**x**t Field
or
Click: 📝 Insert Text Field

In the Insert Text Field dialog box,

Type: **Store Number:**
Choose: **A**ccept

Place the Store Number text field at the left margin of the report in the upper STORE_NUM group section. Italicize and bold the Store Number text field.

Next you want the report to display the database field for the store number. To do this,

Choose: **I**nsert>**D**atabase Field
or
Click: 📊 Insert Database Field
Choose: POSITION–>STORE_NUM>**I**nsert

Place the database field box to the right of the text field in the upper STORE_NUM group section.

Your screen should be similar to Figure 4-16.

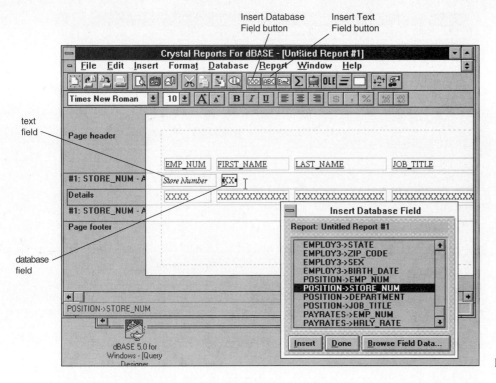

FIGURE 4-16

Close the Insert Database Field dialog box. To see how the report looks, preview the report.

The records for all employees in store #47 are displayed first.

Move through the entire report to view the new layout.

There are four groups of data, one for each store, clearly identified by the descriptive text field.

You feel the grouping of the employees by store number makes the report much clearer. However, you think a second grouping within the store by department would be even better.

Close the Preview window.

To add another group,

Choose: **I**nsert>**G**roup Section

Select the DEPARTMENT field as the field to group on.

Choose: OK

Use the Magnify button to see the full report page.

Your screen should be similar to Figure 4-17.

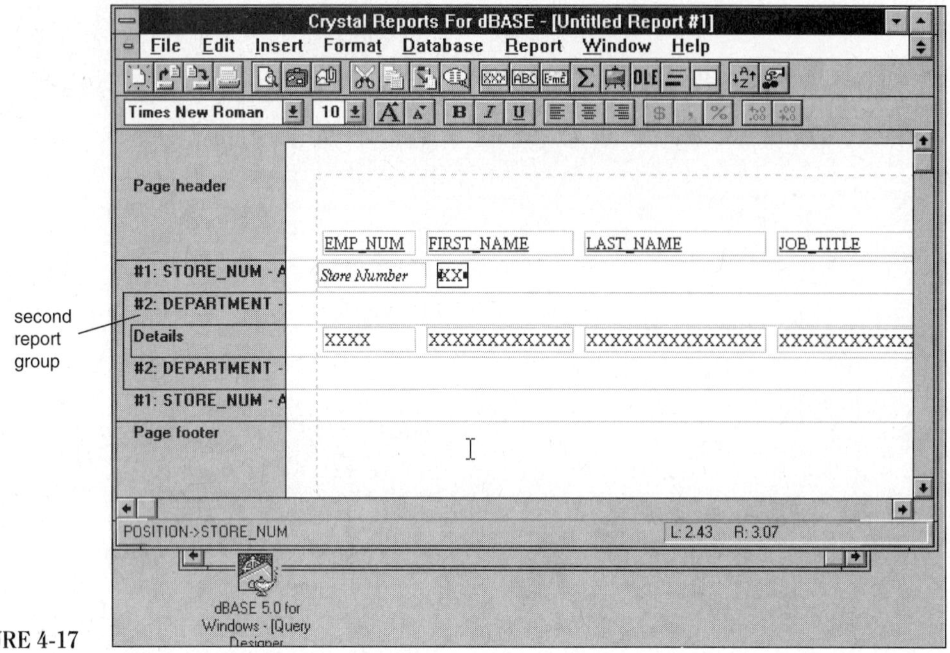

second
report
group

FIGURE 4-17

The DEPARTMENT group section is displayed below the STORE_NUM section in the Report Designer window. When adding group sections to a report, add them so that the largest group is added first, followed by each smaller division.

To add a label to the DEPARTMENT group section,

Choose: Insert>Text Field
or
Click: Insert Text Field

In the Insert Text Field dialog box,

Type: **Department:**
Choose: Accept

Place the Department text field below the word "Number" in the upper DEPARTMENT group section. Italicize and bold the Department text field.

Next you need to insert the database field for the department. To do this,

Choose: Insert>Database Field
or
Click: Insert Database Field
Choose: POSITION–>DEPARTMENT>Insert

Place the database field object after the text field in the upper DEPARTMENT group section. Close the Insert Database Field dialog box.

Your screen should be similar to Figure 4-18.

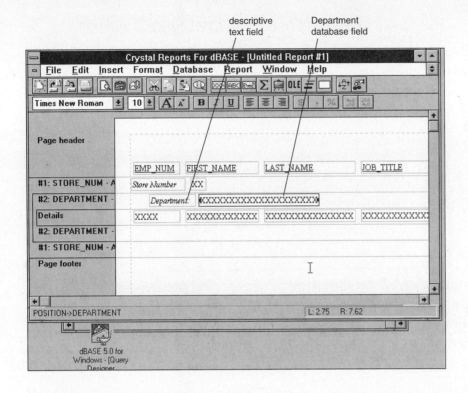

FIGURE 4-18

To see how the report looks now, preview the report. Scroll through the report to see the effect of the grouping by department. When you are done, return to the Report Designer screen.

Enhancing the Report

You would like to add a title to the report that will appear as a header at the top of each page.

Choose:	**I**nsert>Te**x**t Field
or	
Click:	ABC Insert Text Field
Type:	**Monthly Employee Report**
Choose:	**A**ccept

Place the report title at the left margin of the first line in the page header section. You would also like the date displayed below the title.

Choose:	**I**nsert>Special Field>**D**ate

Place the Date field object at the left margin below the report title. Center both the report title and date text fields over the report columns (align the right edge of the text boxes with the last column of data).

DATABASE

Finally, you would like to draw a box around the Store Number group label to make it stand out better.

If necessary, scroll the window so the store number text label is visible.

To add a box,

Choose: Insert>Box

or

Click: ☐ Draw Box

The mouse pointer shape changes to a pencil ✎.

Move the pointer to the Store Number label and position it so that it will be one corner of the box. Click the mouse button to set that position as a corner. Drag the mouse to the diagonally opposite corner. As you do, a box is created. When you release the mouse, the box position is set. Deselect the object.

Your screen should be similar to Figure 4-19.

FIGURE 4-19

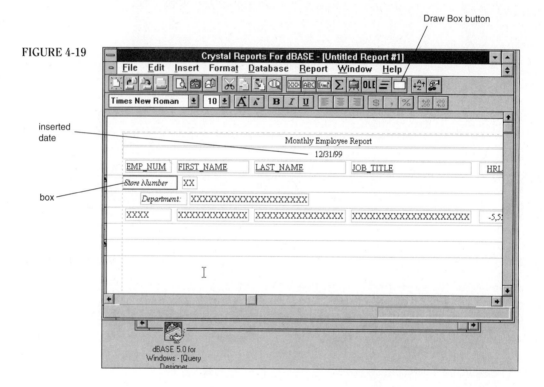

If you need to remove a box, select it and press Delete. However, if there is an object in the box, move the object outside the box first or the object will also be deleted. If you accidentally remove an object, you can recover it if you immediately use the Undo command on the Edit menu.

Preview your changes to the report. Return to the Report Designer window.

The last thing you would like to do is change the column headings to be more descriptive and add blank lines.

Use the Text Field command on the Edit menu or SpeedMenu to make the following changes to the field names:

Field Name	Change To
EMP_NUM	**NUMBER**
FIRST_NAME	**NAME**
JOB_TITLE	**JOB TITLE**
HRLY_RATE	**PAY RATE**

Delete the LAST_NAME field name. Add blank lines above and below the field names and above the data to improve the report's appearance. Preview the report at actual page size.

Your screen should be similar to Figure 4-20.

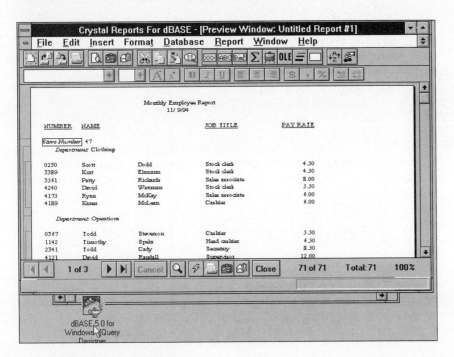

FIGURE 4-20

Return to the Report Designer.

To save the report,

Choose: File>Save As>PAYRATE>OK

Exit the Crystal Reports program. Close the PAYRATES Query Designer window.

Note: If you are running short on lab time, this is an appropriate place to end this session.

Creating a Report with a Calculated Field

The next report you would like to create will display the gross pay by store and department. To create this report, you can use the query you created and saved in Lab 3 as GROSSPAY.

Open the file GROSSPAY.QBE (File>Open>Query). Switch to the Query Designer and, if necessary, maximize the Query Designer window.

The report needs to display the EMP_NUM, STORE_NUM, and DEPARTMENT fields. To modify the query,

■ Place a check mark in the EMP_NUM selection check box in the Employ3 table skeleton.

■ Place a check mark in the STORE_NUM and DEPARTMENT selection check boxes in the Position table skeleton.

■ Remove the check mark from the HRLY_RATE field of the Payrates table skeleton.

Your screen should be similar to Figure 4-21.

FIGURE 4-21

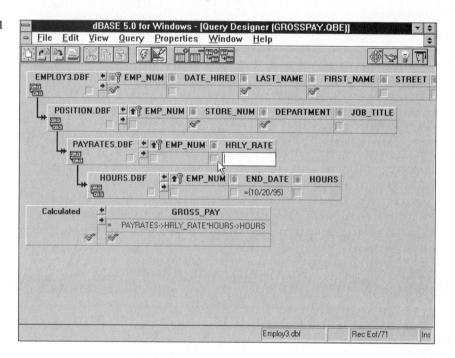

Run the query, then return to the Query Designer window and resave the query.

To create the report,

Choose: File>**N**ew>**R**eport
or
Click: ⬚ New File>**R**eport

Maximize the Report window. Add the fields EMP_NUM, FIRST_NAME, LAST_NAME, and GROSSPAY to the Report Designer window.

Next you will add group sections to group the report on STORE_NUM and DEPARTMENT.

Create a group section for STORE_NUM. Then create a second section for DEPARTMENT. Add text fields and database fields to describe the group sections. Close the Insert Database Field dialog box.

Your screen should be similar to Figure 4-22.

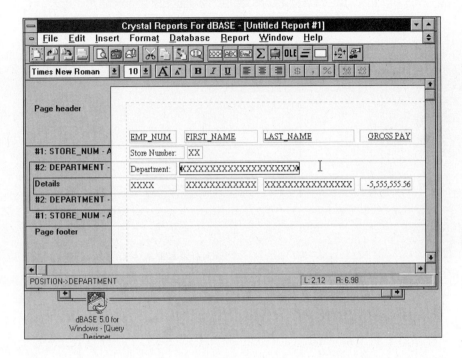

FIGURE 4-22

Preview the report. When you are done, return to the Report Designer window.

Creating Totals

You would like to include a subtotal for each store along with a grand total at the end of the report. To do this, you enter a formula in the appropriate lower group section to sum the values in each group.

First you will enter the formula to display totals for the Store groups. The bottom Store group section will display the subtotal below each group of records.

Move to: GROSS PAY field in the details section

Choose: Insert>Summary Field>Subtotal

The Insert Subtotal dialog box is displayed. To accept the default choice to total by store,

Choose: OK

Your screen should be similar to Figure 4-23.

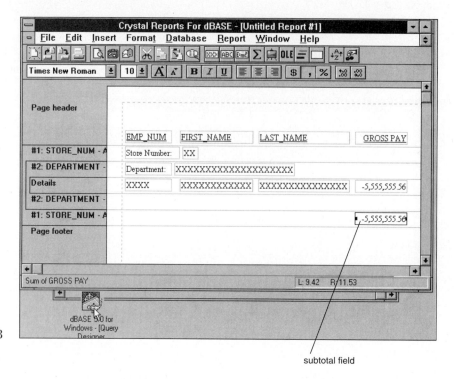

FIGURE 4-23

subtotal field

A subtotal field has been added to the lower Store Number group section.

To create a grand total at the bottom of the report, you need to create a summary field in the bottom report section.

Move to: GROSS PAY field in the details section
Choose: Insert>Summary Field>Grand Total

Notice that the dialog box displays "sum" in the list box. This indicates the program will sum all the gross pay amounts for the entire report.

Choose: OK

A grand total section and field are automatically added to the report above the page footer.

Next you would like to include labels to describe the subtotal and grand total fields. The first label will display the store number. To do this,

Choose: Insert>Text Field
or
Click: 🔤 Insert Text Field
Type: **Store**
Choose: Accept

Place the text field to the left of the gross pay subtotal field, as shown in Figure 4-24.

Your screen should be similar to Figure 4-24.

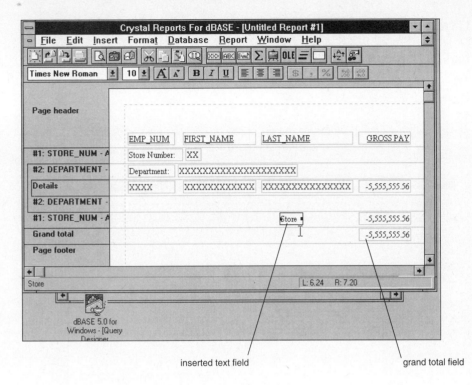

inserted text field   grand total field

FIGURE 4-24

To display the store number following the text label,

Choose:	**I**nsert>**D**atabase Field
or	
Click:	🔲 Insert Database Field
Choose:	POSITION–>STORE_NUM>**I**nsert

Place the Store Number database field to the right of the label "Store" in the bottom STORE_NUM section. Close the Insert Database Field dialog box.

    To add "Grosspay" to the label,

Choose:	**I**nsert>Te**x**t Field
or	
Click:	🔲 Insert Text Field
Type:	**Grosspay**
Choose:	**A**ccept

Place the Grosspay text field to the right of the store number database field in the bottom STORE_NUM group section. Adjust the spacing between the text and field objects on the line if necessary by moving the fields (see Figure 4-25).

Move the Insert Database Field dialog box if it covers the store label.

To move a field, select it and drag it to a new location.

DATABASE

Finally, to add a label to identify the grand total gross pay field,

Choose:	Insert>Text Field
or	
Click:	Insert Text Field
Type:	**Total Grosspay**
Choose:	Accept

Place the field to the left of the total gross pay field in the grand total section. Your screen should be similar to Figure 4-25.

FIGURE 4-25

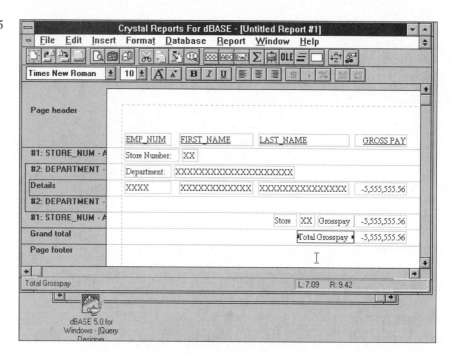

Preview the report. Move to the bottom of the report to see the grand total. When you are done, return to the Report Designer window.

Next, you would like to add page numbers to the page footer to help you keep the report pages in order. To do this,

Choose: Insert>Special Field>**P**age Number

Place the page number on the left margin in the footer section. Center the page number on the page.

The next thing you would like to do is change the column headings to be more descriptive. Using the Text Field command on the Edit menu, make the following changes:

Field Name	Change To
EMP_NUM	**NUMBER**
FIRST_NAME	**NAME**

Delete the LAST_NAME field name. Insert a blank line below the field names.

Changing Margins

You would like the report to print in the center of the page. To do this, you can increase the left margin so that the report prints farther from the left edge of the paper. To change the margin,

Choose: File>Page Margins

The Page Margins dialog box is displayed. The default margins are .25 inch from the edge of the paper. You would like the top and bottom margin to be 1 inch and the left margin to be 2 inches. To change the top margin,

Choose: Top Margin
Type: 1

In a similar manner, change the left margin to 2 and the bottom margin to 1.
You do not need to change the right margin for this report.

Choose: OK

The Report Designer reflects the new margin settings.
The last thing you would like to do is enter a report title.

Choose: Insert>Text Field
or
Click: 🔲 Insert Text Field
Type: **Weekly Employee Gross Pay Report**
Choose: Accept

Place the report title in the report header section of the report. Increase the report title to a font size of 16. Center the title over the report columns. Preview the report.
Save the report design as GROSSPAY. Print the page of the report that displays your name as an employee. Exit the Crystal Reports program. Close the Query Designer window.

DATABASE

Creating a Catalog

Because The Sports Company plans to create database tables of several different types of unrelated information, you want to create a catalog to hold all the tables containing employee information. A **catalog** is a file that contains a list of related files so they can be easily accessed.

To create a catalog,

Choose: File>New

or

Click: New File

Choose: Catalog

> You can also click Catalog and Untitled in the Navigation window.

Your screen should be similar to Figure 4-26.

FIGURE 4-26

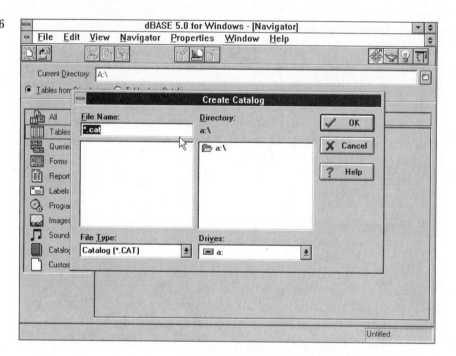

The Create Catalog dialog box is displayed. In the File Name text box, you need to enter a descriptive name for the catalog.

> .CAT is a catalog file extension.

Type: employee

Choose: OK

After a few moments, dBASE displays the Catalog Item Description dialog box. You need to enter a description of the catalog in the text box. Since this catalog will contain information about The Sports Company employees,

Type: **Sports Company Employee Records**
Choose: OK

The description can be up to 80 characters long.

The drive light goes on briefly, and the catalog for your database is saved on the data disk in the drive you specified.

The Catalog window is opened and displayed over the Navigation window. The Catalog window displays the names of all files in the catalog. The title bar displays the catalog name. The description you entered is displayed on the first line of this window. Because this catalog is new, it does not contain any files; therefore, no files are listed in the window except the blank table file named Untitled.

To display the new Catalog window next to the Navigation window that displays the files,

Choose: <u>W</u>indow>Tile <u>V</u>ertically
  ➢   ⇧ Shift + F4

The Navigator window is displayed next to the Catalog window.

Next you want to add the four files you used in this lab to the catalog.

To do this, select the Employ3 table in the Navigator window. Drag the file name to the Catalog window.

The mouse pointer changes to a 🖑.

Release the mouse button.

The Catalog Item Description dialog box is displayed. To add a description for the table, in the Table Description text box,

Type: **Employee Personal data**
Choose: OK

In a similar manner, move the Position, Payrates, and Hours files adding appropriate descriptions.

You can also move the queries and reports you created to the appropriate category in the catalog.

Move the queries and reports you created to the proper category in the new Catalog window. Add appropriate descriptions to each query and report.

Now, when you use dBASE, you can open the Catalog window and quickly locate your related tables.

Exit dBASE and Windows.

Key Terms

Crystal Reports   (DB124)
Report Designer   (DB125)
data type   (DB127)
grouping   (DB140)
catalog   (DB154)

Command Summary

Command	Shortcut	SpeedBar	Action
File>**N**ew>**R**eport			Opens Report Designer window
File>**P**rint>**W**indow		🔲	Displays report as it will be printed
Edit>Te**x**t Field			Edits default text field
Insert>Te**x**t Field		ABC	Adds a text field to report
Forma**t**>**F**ont>**S**ize			Changes size of font
Forma**t**>F**i**eld>**A**lignment		▤,▤,▤	Changes alignment of text in selected object
Report>Record **S**ort Order		↕️	Sorts report by selected field
File>**P**rint>**P**rinter		🖨	Prints a report
Insert>**G**roup Section			Groups report on selected field
Insert>**D**atabase Field		▦	Inserts a field in report
Insert>**B**ox		▢	Draws a box around an object
Insert>Summary Field			Adds a summary total for a numeric field
File>Page Margins			Adjusts size of report margins
Window>Tile **V**ertically	⇧ Shift + F4		Tiles open windows

Matching

1. section	_____	**a.** the section of the report that displays the records of the table
2. data type	_____	**b.** displays report as it will be printed
3. Crystal Reports	_____	**c.** calculated subtotal that prints at bottom of each group
4. summary field	_____	**d.** represents a character data type
5. grouping	_____	**e.** contains information that is printed at top of each page
6. page header	_____	**f.** contains a list of all related files
7. preview	_____	**g.** program used to create custom reports
8. catalog	_____	**h.** divides report into areas
9. details	_____	**i.** classification of data by data that appears in field
10. XXXXX	_____	**j.** organizes and arranges information on a report

Practice Exercises

1. In this problem, you will use the Employ3, Position, and Hours tables that were used in Labs 3 and 4. The Division Manager would like you to create a report to show the number of hours each employee worked, along with the hourly rate grouped by job title.

    a. Create a query from the tables that displays the EMP_NUM, FIRST_NAME, LAST_NAME, JOB_TITLE, and HOURS for the week ending 10/27/95.

    b. Run the query. Return to the Query Designer window and save the query as HOURS.

    c. Create a report using the HOURS query.

    d. Group the report on JOB_TITLE. Add a label to the upper group section. Increase the font size to 12. Add the JOB_TITLE database field after the label.

    e. Create a subtotal that displays the total hours worked in each group. Add a descriptive label before the subtotal.

    f. Create a grand total for the overall number of hours worked. Add a descriptive label before the grand total.

You would like to change the display of the Hours column and totals to be displayed with one decimal place instead of two. The Field command on the Format menu or the SpeedMenu can be used to change the display of decimal places.

    g. Change the number of decimal places for the Hours column from 1.00 to 1.0.

    h. Enter an appropriate report title centered on the report. Display the date centered below the title. Add blank lines as needed to enhance the appearance of the report.

    i.   Print the last page of the report. Save the report as WKLYHRS.

2.   To complete this problem, you must have completed Practice Exercise 4 in Lab 3. Rebecca would like you to create a report using the tables Photoinv and Photoqty.

    a.   Create a report using the Photoinv and Photoqty tables that shows the item number, item name, and quantity on hand. Group the report by reorder point. Add an appropriate title. Print the report.

    b.   Create a report showing the total wholesale price of the inventory on hand. Add the appropriate fields for this type of report. Add an appropriate title. Print the report.

    c.   Create a report of your choice using data from both tables. Group the report and display totals as appropriate. Add an appropriate title. Print the report.

3.   To complete this problem, you must have completed Practice Exercise 3 in Lab 2. As inventory control manager of The Gift Center, you would like to create some month-end reports. Using the Gifts and Supplier tables, complete the following steps.

    a.   Create a report that displays the suppliers and the products they supply. Print the report.

    b.   Create a query that displays the products and the price. Also create a new column that increases the price by 5 percent. Create a report from the query. Print the report.

    c.   Create a report of your choice using the data from both tables. Group the report and display totals as appropriate.

4.   Aaron has accepted a position with The Sports Equipment Center. He would like to create a database to help him keep track of the store's inventory, suppliers, and orders placed. The inventory table should include information such as the item number, description, supplier number, quantity on hand, and retail price. The supplier table should include information about the supplier such as the supplier number, name, and address. The orders table should include information such as the item number, quantity ordered, supplier number, date ordered, and wholesale price per item ordered.

    a.   Create the three tables using appropriate field names. Include key fields as needed. Enter 10 records into each table. Enter your name in the description field of one of the records.

    b.   Create a report showing the item number and description in alphabetical order by description. Print the report.

    c.   Create a report showing the orders placed. Include the item number, item description, and total price of the order. Group the report by supplier. Include a total to show the total price of all outstanding orders. Print the report.

    d.   Create a report showing the total wholesale and retail value of the inventory on hand. Include the item number, description, and wholesale and retail prices. Print the report.

5.   To complete this problem, you must have completed Practice Exercise 5 in Lab 3. Create three reports using the tables. At least one of the reports should have two groups. Total the report by the major group and include a grand total at the end of the report. Print the reports.

Final Project

This project is designed to reinforce your knowledge of the database features used in the dBASE labs. You will also be expected to use the Help feature to learn more about advanced features available in dBASE.

Marianne Virgili is the Director of the Glenwood Springs Chamber Resort Association. The Director has asked you to create a relational database of the Chamber members.

Part I

In this section you will create the tables that will make up your database. Refer to the section in Lab 1 for information on planning a database.

a. On paper, design a table to hold the Chamber members' information. The table should include a membership number, the business name, address (including street, city, state, and zip code), a telephone number, and contact name.

b. On paper, design a table to hold the types of businesses that belong to the Chamber of Commerce. This table should include the membership number, type of business, and the number of employees the business employs. (Hint: Companies employ a single number of employees, for example, "1" or "50" not "1 to 50.")

c. On paper, design a table to hold the dues payments for the Chamber members. This table should include the membership number, date the payment is due, and the amount of the payment. The amount of payment is based on the number of employees the company employs. The companies are divided into three categories: small (1 to 20 employees), medium (21 to 60 employees), and large (61 or more employees). Small companies pay dues of $200, medium companies pay $300, and large companies pay $500.

d. From your paper designs, create the three tables. Create indexes on the common fields. Save the tables using appropriate names.

e. Create a customized form for each of the tables.

f. Use the customized forms to enter 25 members into the tables. (Add yourself as one of the company names.) Be sure to enter the same membership number for each individual member so that the records can be joined in queries and reports. Also remember that the number of employees determines the payment amount due.

g. Create a catalog to hold the three tables and move them to the proper category in the catalog.

Part II

You will use the tables you created in Part I to create queries on the data.

a. Create a query that shows the membership number, member name, and the city. Sort the query by city. Print the query.

b. Create a query that shows the types of businesses that belong to the Chamber of Commerce, along with the name, membership number, and number of employees they employ. Sort the query by type of business and membership number. Save the query as MEMTYPE. Print the query.

c. Create a query for the members that employ more than 50 employees. Display any fields you feel would be appropriate in a report that contains this data. Print the query.

Part III

a. Using Crystal Reports, create a report that shows the due date for all the members whose payments are due from the current date to two months from now. Include any fields you feel would be appropriate for this report. Use groups if necessary and add an appropriate title. Print the report.

b. Open the saved query MEMTYPE. Create a report from the query. Group the report by type of business. Print the report.

c. Create a report that groups the companies by categories: small, medium, and large. Total the dues payments for each group and display the percentage for each group. Include the member's name and any other fields that you feel are appropriate. Print the report.

dBASE 5.0 for Windows

Glossary of Key Terms

Attribute: Character display changed by adding bold, underlines, and italics.

Calculated field: A field that is created from one or more other fields.

Catalog: A group of related files.

Checks: Evaluations performed automatically by dBASE to ensure that the data entered into a field meets certain requirements or standards.

Child table: In a multitable relationship, the table whose records are dependent on those in the parent table.

Command window: Displays the dBASE language commands that execute when actions are performed.

Comparison operator: Used to generate logical results. The operators are > (greater than), < (less than), = (equal to), <> or # (not equal to), <= (less than or equal to), and >= (greater than or equal to).

Condition field: The text space in the query skeleton where field conditions are entered.

Crystal Reports: Program used to create custom reports, lists, and form letters using data from dBASE tables.

Data type: Attribute for a field that determines what type of data it can contain.

Database: An organized collection of related information.

Design surface: The background of a form.

Desktop: The area of the dBASE screen between the SpeedBar at the top and the status bar at the bottom, where images are displayed in windows.

Entry field: The space on a form where field values are displayed.

Field: A single category of data in a table, the values of which appear in a column.

Field selection check box: The box in the query skeleton that when checked marks the fields to be displayed in the view.

DATABASE

Field type: Defines the type of data a field can contain.

Field value: The specific data contained in a field.

Field width: The maximum number of characters that can be entered in the field.

Font: Size and style of characters.

Freeze: Restricts editing to the selected field.

Grid: A matrix of dots used to help place items on a form.

Grouping: In a report, a set of records that have the same value in one or more fields, or fall within a range of values, or are grouped into a fixed number of records.

Index: Changing the display order of the fields in a table without changing the structure of the table.

Index field: One or more fields in a table that controls the order of the records.

Key field: See *index field*.

Link: A logical association between two tables based on matching values in common fields.

Logical AND: In a query, when multiple conditions are entered on the same line, all conditions must be met by a record for the record to appear in the view. To create an AND condition within a field, separate the conditions with a comma.

Logical OR: In a query, when multiple conditions are entered on separate lines, either of the conditions must be met by a record for the record to appear in the View.

Menu bar: The top line of the dBASE screen containing commands relevant to the current mode.

Mode: The current state of operation of the program. For example, in Edit mode you can change the contents of a field value.

Multiselect: To select multiple objects to be manipulated. This is only available if you have a mouse.

Multitable query: Query that contains data from more than one table.

Multivalued relationship: A relationship between linked tables in which there is one record in one table that corresponds to one or many records in another table. Also called a one-to-many relationship.

Natural order: The order records were entered into a table.

Navigator: The window used to access and organize your database files.

Object: A window element that has properties and that can be selected, moved, and sized, such as text boxes, entry fields, and spin boxes.

Operator: A symbol that represents an operation to be performed on a value, such as + for addition.

Pack: The process of permanently removing records marked for deletion from a table.

Parent table: In a multitable relationship, the table you are linking from.

Property: An attribute of an object.

Query: A question you ask about the data stored in dBASE tables.

Query by example or **QBE:** A way of designing queries without writing program code by adding fields to the query skeleton.

Query skeleton: Fields displayed in the Query Designer window.

Record: Each row of a dBASE table is one record. Each record is a group of related fields.

Record number: A unique number that identifies each record in a table.

Relational database: A database in which you can define a relationship between tables by creating one or more links based on common fields.

Relational operator: See *comparison operator*.

Relationship: Common data between two or more table files.

Report Designer: Used to control the layout of the report.

Reserved word: A word that has special meaning to dBASE.

Ruler bar: The horizontal and vertical rulers displayed in the Form Designer to assist with the placement of objects in the window.

Selection handles: Black boxes surrounding a selected object.

Single-valued relationship: A relationship between linked tables in which there is one record in one table that corresponds to one record in another table. Also called a one-to-one relationship.

Size: Height of characters.

Sort: To arrange the records in a table based on the values in one or more fields.

SpeedBar: The set of buttons and tools for frequently performed tasks displayed under the main menu.

SpeedMenu: Displays menu options for a specific screen element. Opened by using the mouse and the right mouse button.

Spin box: Feature used to enter numeric values either by clicking the appropriate spin box button or using the ⬆ or ⬇ keys to increase or decrease the number.

Status bar: The bottom line of the screen that displays messages and mode indicators.

Structure: The arrangement of fields in a table.

Tab dialog box: Dialog box that contains tabs across the bottom that are used to access different folders of related options.

Tabbing order: The order in which the highlight moves based on how the fields were placed on a form.

Table: A structure made up of records and fields used to hold data.

Text: Descriptive elements consisting of alphanumeric characters that can be edited.

Typeface: Refers to the different designs of type, such as Times New Roman and Courier.

User interface: The features in dBASE that allow you to interact with the program; for example: menus, SpeedBar buttons, dialog boxes, and other graphical elements.

View: The output dBASE displays as a result of a query.

Wildcard operator: The symbols * and ? used to locate a pattern of characters.

DATABASE

Summary of Selected dBASE 5.0 for Windows Commands

Command	Shortcut	SpeedBar	Action
Table Menu			
File>**N**ew		⬚	Creates a new file
File>**N**ew>**Q**uery		⬚	Opens Query Designer
File>**N**ew>**F**orm		⬚	Creates new form
File>**N**ew>**R**eport			Opens Report Designer window
File>**S**ave	Ctrl + S	⬚	Saves file using same path and file name
File>**P**rint	Ctrl + P	⬚	Prints file
File>**P**rint>**W**indow		⬚	Displays report as it will be printed
File>**P**rint>**P**rinter		⬚	Prints a report
File>E**x**it	Alt + F4		Exits program
Edit>**U**ndo	Ctrl + Z		Cancels last action
View>**T**able Records	F2	⬚	View used to view, add, and edit records in a table
View>**B**rowse Layout	F2	⬚	Default record display
View>**C**olumnar Layout	F2	⬚	Displays a single record at a time with field names as a vertical list
View>**F**orm Layout	F2	⬚	Displays records as a printed form with field names displayed above field values
Table>**F**ind Records	Ctrl + F	⬚	Locates records in file
Table>**T**able Utilities>**M**anage Indexes			Applies and modifies indexes
Table>**T**able Utilities>**P**ack Records			Erases marked files
Table>**T**able Utilities>**S**ort Records			Arranges records into a new file
Table>**A**dd Records	Ctrl + A	⬚	Adds new record
Table>**D**elete Selected Record	Ctrl + U		Marks selected record for deletion
Table>**P**revious Record	↑	◀	Moves to previous record
Table>**N**ext Record	↓	▶	Moves to next record
Table>Pre**v**ious Page	Page Up	⏪	Moves to previous page
Table>Ne**x**t Page	Page Down	⏩	Moves to next page
Table>T**o**p Record	Ctrl + Page Up	⏮	Moves to top record
Table>Botto**m** Record	Ctrl + Page Down	⏭	Moves to bottom record
Properties>**T**able Records Window>**F**reeze			Freezes and unfreezes field columns
Window>**1** Navigator		⬚	Switches to Navigator window

Command	Shortcut	SpeedBar	Action
Table Designer Menu			
Structure>**I**nsert Field	Ctrl + N		Inserts new field in Design layout view
Form Designer Menu			
View>**F**orm	F2		Displays table in Form layout
View>**O**bject Properties			Changes properties associated with an object
F**o**rm>**A**dd Records	Ctrl + A		Adds a new record and enters data into it
Query Designer Menu			
View>Query **R**esults	F2	⚡	Displays results of a query
View>Query **D**esign	⇧ Shift + F2	✎	Displays design of a query
Query>**A**dd Table	Ctrl + A	▦	Adds table to query
Query>**R**emove Selected Table		▤	Removes selected table from query
Query>**S**et Relation		▦	Defines relation between tables
Query>Create Calculated **F**ield			Inserts a calculated field
Report Designer Menu			
File>Page Margins			Adjusts size of report margins
Edit>Te**x**t Field			Edits default text field
Insert>**D**atabase Field		⊠	Inserts a field in report
Insert>Te**x**t Field		ABC	Adds a text field to report
Insert>Summary Field			Adds a summary total for a numeric field
Insert>**B**ox		▭	Draws a box around an object
Insert>Special Field			Adds a predefined field
Insert>**G**roup Section			Groups a report on selected field
Forma**t**>**F**ont>**S**ize			Changes size of font
Forma**t**>**F**ield>**A**lignment		▤,▤,▤	Changes alignment of text in selected object
Report>Record **S**ort Order		↓²↑	Sorts report by selected field
Window>Tile **V**ertically	⇧ Shift + F4		Tiles open windows

DATABASE

Alert box, DB25
AND, logical, DB98-100
Ascending order, DB62-63, DB65, DB105
Attributes of type, DB115

Binary field type, DB16
Boldface, in reports, DB135
Boxes, adding to reports, DB146
Brackets, for query conditions, DB95
Browse layout, DB30-31
Buttons:
    Add Field, DB61
    Add Record, DB24, DB31
    Add Table, DB103
    Align Center, DB136
    Bottom Record, DB46
    Browse Layout, DB30, DB33
    Columnar Layout, DB30
    Design Query, DB94
    Draw Box, DB146
    Find Records, DB55
    First Record, DB46
    Form Layout, DB30
    Insert Database Field, DB142
    Insert Text Field, DB134
    Magnify, DB137-138
    Modify Table, DB57, DB101
    Navigator, DB100
    New File, DB11
    New Query, DB90
    Next Page, DB46
    Next Record, DB46
    Open, DB45
    Preview, DB129
    on Preview status bar, DB131
    Previous Page, DB46
    Previous Record, DB46
    Print, DB34
    Remove Table, DB113
    Run Form, DB118
    Run Query, DB92

Buttons (continued):
    Run Table, DB102
    Save, DB21
    Set Relation, DB104
    Sort Order, DB137
    SpeedBar, DB11, DB23, DB28, DB46, DB91
    Tool, DB115
    Top Record, DB46
    View Table Data, DB22

Calculated fields, DB109-112
    in reports, DB148-149
Case-sensitive searching, DB50, DB105
Catalogs, creating, DB154-155
Character field type, DB16
    and query conditions, DB95
    sorting order for, DB62
Checks, data, DB25
Child tables, DB101
Color, on forms, DB116
Columnar layout, DB30-31
    navigating in, DB31
Columns:
    editing headings for, DB131-132
    moving, DB93-94
Command window, DB9
Commands:
    Edit>Text Field, DB131
    Edit>Undo, DB56-57
    File>Exit, DB14
    File>New, DB11-12
    File>New>Form, DB71
    File>New>Query, DB90
    File>New>Report, DB124
    File>Open, DB45
    File>Page Margins, DB153
    File>Print, DB34
    File>Print>Printer, DB138
    File>Print>Window, DB129
    File>Save, DB21

Commands (continued):
    File>Save As, DB21
    Form>Add Records, DB82
    Format>Field>Alignment, DB136
    Format>Font>Size, DB135
    Insert>Box, DB146
    Insert>Database Field, DB142
    Insert>Group Section, DB141
    Insert>Special Field>Date, DB145
    Insert>Special Field>Page Number, DB152
    Insert>Summary Field, DB149-150
    Insert>Text Field, DB134
    Properties>Desktop, DB52
    Properties>Desktop>Deleted, DB54
    Properties>Table Records Window>Freeze, DB59-60
    Query>Add Table, DB103
    Query>Create Calculated Field, DB109
    Query>Remove Selected Table, DB113
    Query>Set Relation, DB104
    Report>Record Sort Order, DB137
    Structure>Insert Field, DB58
    Table>Add Records, DB24, DB31
    Table>Bottom Record, DB28
    Table>Delete Selected Record, DB52
    Table>Find Records, DB55
    Table>Next Page, DB28
    Table>Next Record, DB28
    Table>Previous Page, DB28
    Table>Previous Record, DB28
    Table>Replace Records, DB49
    Table>Table Utilities>Manage Indexes, DB66

DATABASE

Commands (continued):
  Table>Table Utilities>Pack
    Records, DB53
  Table>Table Utilities>Recall
    Records, DB53
  Table>Table Utilities>Sort
    Records, DB61
  Table>Top Record, DB28
  View>Browse Layout, DB33
  View>Columnar Layout, DB31
  View>Form, DB81, DB118
  View>Form Layout, DB30
  View>Object Properties, DB77
  View>Query Design, DB94
  View>Query Results, DB92
  View>Table Records, DB22
  View>Table Structure,
    DB57, DB101
  Window>Controls, DB79
  Window>Form Designer, DB80
  Window>1 Navigator, DB100
  Window>Properties, DB80
  Window>Tile Vertically, DB155
Comparison operators, querying
  with, DB97-98
Condition field, DB91
Controls window, DB79-80
Crystal Reports:
  adding boxes to, DB146
  adding date to, DB145
  adding text fields to, DB134-135
  aligning objects in, DB136
  calculated fields in, DB148-149
  changing column headings
    in, DB147
  changing margins in, DB153
  data types in, DB127
  defined, DB5, DB124
  deleting fields in, DB127
  editing text fields in, DB131-134
  grouping in, DB140-145
  headers and footers in,
    DB125, DB130
  moving around in, DB131
  multitable, DB138-140
  page numbers in, DB152
  positioning fields in, DB126-129
  previewing, DB129-131

Crystal Reports (continued):
  sorting in, DB137-138
  totals in, DB149-153
Current field, DB29
Current record, DB29
Customized forms, DB70-73
  entering data in, DB81-82

Data:
  automatic checks of, DB25
  editing, DB47-49
  entering in forms, DB81-82
  entering in tables, DB22-29
  as field values, DB24
  types of, in reports, DB127
Databases:
  advantages of using, DB4
  defined, DB3, DB4, DB9
  planning, DB10-11
  relational, DB3, DB5, DB9
  See also Tables
Date field type:
  checking data for, DB24-25
  defined, DB16, DB18
  inserting in reports, DB145
  and query conditions, DB95
  sorting order for, DB63
dBASE 5.0 for Windows:
  exiting, DB35
  loading, DB7-8
  windows for, DB8-9
Deleting:
  with Backspace, DB15
  boxes in reports, DB146
  defined, DB4
  field names in reports,
    DB132-133
  objects on forms, DB75
  records, DB52-54
Descending order, DB62, DB105
Design surface on forms, DB73
Desktop, DB9
Dialog boxes:
  Create Catalog, DB154
  Desktop Properties, DB53
  Edit an Expression, DB67-68
  Find Records, DB55-56
  Font, DB116
  Form Expert, DB71-72,
    DB113-115
  Insert Database Field,
    DB125-126, DB143

Dialog boxes (continued):
  Modify Index, DB67
  Print Records, DB34
  Properties, DB77-78
  Replace Records, DB50
  Save Table, DB21
  Sort Records, DB61
  tab, DB53
Dollar sign, and memo fields, DB95
Dragging objects, DB76
Drives, setting default, DB22

Editing, DB4
  deleting, DB15
  expressions, DB67-68
  by replacing values, DB49-51
  text fields in Cyrstal Reports,
    DB131-133
  undoing, DB56
Entry field objects, DB74
Exclusive use of files, DB53-54
Exiting dBASE, DB35
Expressions, editing, DB67-68
Extensions, file name:
  .cat, DB154
  .dbf, DB21

Field selection check box, DB91
Field type, DB16
Field values, DB24
Fields:
  adding to reports, DB134-135
  adding to structure, DB58
  calculated, DB109-112
  changing width of, DB20
  condition, DB91
  current, DB29
  defined, DB4, DB9
  freezing, DB59-60
  index, DB17
  key, DB17, DB62
  naming, DB21
  planning, DB11
  position in reports, DB126
  properties of, DB13
  types of, DB16
  width of, DB17-20
File names, DB21-22
  .cat extension, DB154
  .dbf extension, DB21

Files:
catalog, DB154-155
defined, DB5
exclusive use of, DB53-54
linking, DB3, DB10
naming, DB21-22
opening, DB45
types of, DB12, DB44
Float field type, DB16
Fonts, changing, DB115-116
Form Designer window, DB73
Form layout, DB30
Forms:
adding objects to, DB79-81
changing color of, DB116
changing properties of, DB77-79
creating customized, DB70-82
displaying, DB118
entering data in, DB81-82
multitable, DB113-118
using rulers on, DB79
Freezing fields, DB59-60
Function keys:
Help (F1), DB13
View (F2), DB30-31

Grid on Form Designer, DB73
Grouping reports, DB140-145

Help, using, DB13-14

Icons:
Command window, DB9
dBASE for Windows group , DB7
dBASE for Windows
program, DB8
Index field, DB17
Indexed tables, DB17
updating, DB69-70
Indexing tables, DB61, DB65-69

Key expression, DB67
Key field, DB17
Keys:
(Backspace), DB15
(Delete), DB48
(←Enter), DB18
for moving insertion point, DB47
(Page Up), (Page Down), DB31
(Tab ⇄), DB18, DB31

Layouts:
Browse, DB30-31
Columnar, DB30-31
Form, DB30
Linking tables:
defined, DB3, DB10, DB101
for querying, DB100-105
Logical AND and OR, DB98-100
Logical field type, DB16
and query conditions, DB95

Margins in reports, DB153
Memo field type, DB16
and query conditions, DB95
sorting order for, DB63
Menu bar, DB9
Menus:
Form Designer, DB73
Query Designer, DB90-91
SpeedMenu, DB49
Table, DB23
Modes, defined, DB9
Multiselecting objects, DB76
Multitable forms, DB113-118
Multitable queries, DB101
Multitable reports, DB138-140
Multivalued relationships, DB112

Naming:
fields, DB15
files, DB21-22
Natural order of records,
DB61, DB105
Navigator, using, DB43-46
Numeric field type, DB16
and query conditions, DB95
sorting order for, DB62

Objects on forms:
adding, DB79-81
aligning, DB136
entry field, DB74
multiselecting, DB76
properties of, DB77-78
selecting and moving, DB73-77
spin boxes as, DB73-74
tabbing order of, DB75
text, DB73-74
OLE field type, DB16

Operators:
comparison, DB97
query, DB95
OR, logical, DB98-100

Packing records, DB52
Page headers and footers, DB125
Page numbers in reports, DB152
Parent tables, DB101
Path, setting, DB22
Periods, for logical queries, DB95
Printing:
tables, DB34-35
views, DB94
Properties of objects, DB77
Properties window, DB80

Query by example (QBE), DB90
Query Designer window, DB90-92
Querying:
with comparison operators,
DB97-98
defined, DB90
for exact match, DB106
with logical AND and OR,
DB98-100
with operators, DB95
and reserved words, DB95
three tables, DB107-108
two tables, DB100-105
with wildcards, DB94-96
Quitting dBASE, DB35
Quotations marks, for query
conditions, DB95

Records:
adding in forms, DB81-82
current, DB29
defined, DB5, DB9
deleting, DB52-54
finding, DB54-57
moving between, DB28,
DB31, DB46
in natural order, DB61
numbers for, DB24

Records (continued):
    packing, DB52
    replacing values in, DB49-51
    sorting, DB61-64
    viewing, DB30-34, DB45
Relation, defined, DB9
Relational databases, DB3, DB5, DB9
Report Designer, DB125
Reports. *See* Crystal Reports
Reserved words, DB95
Ruler bars, DB73, DB79

Saving:
    changes to structure, DB58
    and Save/Save As commands,
        DB21
    table structure, DB21-22
Searching:
    defined, DB5
    and replacing, DB49-51
Selection bar, DB24
Selection handles on objects, DB74
Single-valued relationships, DB111
Size of printed characters, DB115
Skeleton, table structure, DB91
Sorting:
    in Crystal Reports, DB137-138
    defined, DB5
    drawbacks of, DB64
    order for, DB62-63
    records, DB61-64
SpeedBar, DB9
    button for, DB11
    buttons on, DB23, DB28, DB46
    Crystal Reports, DB125
    Form Designer, DB73
    Query Designer, DB91
SpeedMenu, DB49
Spin boxes, DB73-74
Status bar, DB9
    buttons, on Preview window,
        DB131
Structure of tables:
    defining, DB12-13, DB15-20
    restructuring, DB57-59

Tab dialog box, DB53
Tabbing order of objects, DB75
Table Designer, DB12
Table Structure window, DB12
Tables:
    child, DB101
    defined, DB9
    defining structure of, DB12
    indexed, DB17
    indexing, DB61, DB65-69
    inputting fields for, DB16-20
    linking, DB3, DB10, DB100-105
    locating information in, DB54-57
    moving in, DB18, DB20, DB28,
        DB29, DB31, DB46
    and multivalued relationships,
        DB112
    parent, DB101
    planning fields for, DB11
    printing, DB34-35
    properties of, DB13
    querying three, DB107-108
    querying two, DB100-105
    restructuring, DB57-59
    saving structure of, DB21-22
    and single-valued relationships,
        DB111
    skeleton of structure, DB91
    sorting, DB5, DB61-64
    structure of, DB12-13, DB15-20
    updating indexed, DB69-70
Text objects on forms, DB73-74
    adding, DB80
    editing, DB131-133
Text tool, DB80
Tiling windows, DB155
Totals, adding in reports, DB149-153
Typeface, for forms, DB115

Undoing edits, DB56
Unmarking records for deletion,
    DB53
Updating indexed tables, DB69-70
User interface, DB9

Values, field, DB24
    replacing, DB49-51

View:
    defined, DB90
    printing, DB94
Viewing records, DB30-34

Width of fields, DB17-20
    changing, DB20
Wildcard operators, querying with,
    DB94-96
Windows:
    Command, DB9
    Controls, DB79-80
    Crystal Reports for dBASE,
        DB124
    dBASE application, DB8-9
    Form Designer, DB73
    Help, DB14
    Navigator, DB8, DB9, DB44
    Properties, DB80
    Query Designer, DB90-92
    Query Results, DB93
    Table Records, DB23, DB45
    Table Structure, DB12-13
    tiling, DB155
Windows (Microsoft):
    Program Manager, DB7
    starting, DB7
    Table Structure, DB12
Words, reserved, DB95

NOTES

DB172
Notes